NAKED SALES

HOW TO BECOME A SALES PROPHET IN YOUR HOMETOWN

Robert Andolšek

NAKED SALES - HOW TO BECOME A SALES PROPHET IN YOUR HOMETOWN

Copyright © 2018 Robert Andolšek
All rights reserved.

ISBN-13: 978-1985741416
ISBN-10: 1985741415

Credits

Editor: Dominik Božič
Translation: Maja Davis
Cover & Design: Dominik Božič

NAKED SALES

HOW TO BECOME A SALES PROPHET IN YOUR HOMETOWN

ROBERT ANDOLŠEK

»Anything that won't sell, I don't want to invent. Its sale is proof of utility, and utility is success.«

Thomas Edison

First and foremost I would like to thank Mojca and my two inspirations, Leo and Teo Tim.

I would also like to thank my most constructive critic, Dominik, and Larisa - I couldn't have done it without you.

Thanks also to my father Stane and niece Maja for their "beta" reading and constructive suggestions.

I would like to express a special thank you to all of you who are part of my business life. I love you all and I couldn't do it without you.

Credit for everything that is good in this book goes to those who I mentioned or can be recognised in these pages. I have had several teachers in my life who helped me with their suggestions, but the best teachers were those whose mistakes I was able to learn from. I have even "forgotten" to repeat some of those mistakes.

Responsibility for any mistakes in this book is all mine -
"I'm only human, born to make mistakes"
(Human, The human league, album Crash, September 1986).

TABLE OF CONTENTS

THE CURTAIN OF HISTORY 1
FOREWORD 3
INTRODUCTION 5
1. Setting Goals 9
1.1 WISHES AND ACTIVITIES. 9
1.2 ACHIEVING GOALS 10
1.3 TALENTS, KNOWLEDGE AND SKILLS 10
1.4 PRACTICAL PART: DISCOVER YOUR TALENTS
     11
1.5 IN BRIEF: SETTING GOALS 19
2. The Basics of Sales 21
2.1 SALES IS HELPING 22
2.2 PRODUCT OR SOLUTION 22
     What do you sell? 22
     Why is the term product so unacceptable? . 23
     The naked truth: An example of selling solutions
     24
2.3 MISSION 26
2.4 SALESPERSON 26
     Preparation for a meeting. 27
     Salesperson in practice 38
     The salesperson in everyday life 40
     The salesperson and family 42
2.5 THE SALESPERSON'S TALENTS, KNOWLEDGE
     AND SKILLS 45
     Tools for recognising the salesperson's talent
     46
     What am I good at as a salesperson 47
2.6 TYPES OF SALESPEOPLE 47
     Stereotypes 49
2.7 DEVELOPING THE SALESPERSON'S
     STRATEGIES 50

2.8   SALESPEOPLE'S MOTIVATION. 52
      Salespeople's self-motivation 54
      Motivating others 55
2.9   STORYTELLING - THE BASIS OF A GOOD SALESPERSON. 56
2.10 THE NAKED TRUTH: EXAMPLES OF STORYTELLING IN A GIVEN SALES SITUATION 57
2.11 IMPORTANT SALESPERSON'S SKILLS - TEN RULES. 57
2.12 PRACTICAL PART: THE SALESPERSON IN PRACTICE. 59
2.13 IN BRIEF: THE BASICS OF SALES 61

3. Sales Tools. 63
3.1   DEVELOPMENT OF A BUSINESS IDEA
THE REQUIRED KNOWLEDGE OF EVERY SALESPERSON. 63
. . . . 64
      Practical tool for developing a business idea 64
      Tools for developing a business idea. 64
      Naked truth: An example of using tools to develop a business idea. 67
      A good idea no one wants to buy is just a good idea 68
3.2   ENTREPRENEURIAL STAGES. 68
      Pitfalls of entrepreneurial stages 69
3.3   BRAINSTORMING. 74
3.4   ANALYSIS TOOLS. 75
3.5   IT'S ALSO GOOD TO TALK TO YOURSELF . . 77
      The naked truth: An example of using sales tools 78
3.6   PRACTICAL PART: SALES TOOLS. 81
3.7   IN BRIEF: SALES TOOLS. 82

4. There Are No Sales Without Clients. 83
4.1   WHO ARE YOUR BUYERS. 83
4.2   SALES VIA AGENTS AND DISTRIBUTORS . . . 85
4.3   WHO IS AN AGENT AND WHO IS A DISTRIBUTOR 86

	The naked truth: An example of business communication with a representative of a company 88
4.4	BUYERS' AREAS 89
4.5	BUYER'S COMMERCIAL PHILOSOPHY...... 89
	The naked truth: Example of our solutions' field of use 90
4.6	HOW TO INTENSIVELY LOOK FOR CLIENTS . 90
4.7	FIRST CONTACT WITH A CLIENT 91
	The naked truth: An example of first contact with a buyer 92
4.8	SELLING COMPLEX SOLUTIONS AND CLIENTS 93
	First meeting 93
	Preparation for a second meeting 94
4.9	PRACTICAL PART: CLIENTS. 95
4.10	IN BRIEF: CLIENTS. 96

5. Sales Closing 97

5.1	PRACTICE = SUCCESSFUL SALES. 97
	Observing the client 98
	Adapting to the client................... 101
	Pain 101
	Preparing for objections 102
	Sales is not a scam 104
5.2	CLOSING THE SALE IS THE MOST IMPORTANT PART 105
5.3	SALES STEPS TO REACH CLOSING 106
	The naked truth: An example of sales steps 109
5.4	THE SALES CYCLE IN STEPS............ 109
	Sales cycle 112
5.5	PRACTICAL PART: SALES CLOSING....... 113
5.6	IN BRIEF: SALES CLOSING............... 114

6. Cross-Selling 115

6.1	WHAT IS CROSS-SELLING?............... 115
6.2	DON'T SELL, ADVISE.................... 116
	The naked truth: An example of giving advice 117

6.3 FORCING THE BUYER................118
   The naked truth: Examples of forcing the buyer in a given sales situation...............118
6.4 CROSS-SELLING MEANS TRUSTING YOURSELF AND THE SOLUTION YOU ARE SELLING................................119
6.5 CROSS-SELLING SUPPLEMENTS THE SALESPERSON'S PROMISES............120
6.6 AFTER-SALES SUPPORT.................121
   The naked truth: An example of after-sales support................................121
6.7 PRACTICAL PART: CROSS-SELLING.......122
6.8 IN BRIEF: CROSS-SELLING..............123
7. You Can't Do It All on Your Own..........125
7.1 TIME......................................125
7.2 SALES PROCESSES AND WORK DISTRIBUTION.........................126
7.3 DEVELOPMENT OF THE SALES DEPARTMENT 127
7.4 LEADERSHIP.............................127
   What is leadership......................128
   Five-level leadership...................132
   Is leadership a mistake.................133
   Leadership in practice 134
7.5 BOARD MEETING AND MEETING.........136
   What is a meeting and what is a board meeting 136
   Why is a board meeting important for the company...............................137
   Presiding over a board meeting...........139
   Presiding over a board meeting following a process................................140
   Common mistakes in presiding over a board meeting................................142
   Solutions to the mistakes in presiding over a board meeting........................143
   Other participants should also have a say .146
7.6 PRACTICAL PART: YOU CAN'T DO

	EVERYTHING ON YOUR OWN............147
7.7	IN BRIEF: YOU CAN'T DO EVERYTHING ON YOUR OWN............................148

8. Company Management....................149
- 8.1   COMPANY MANAGEMENT................149
- 8.2   COMPANY DEVELOPMENT STRATEGY.....150
- 8.3   A WORKING MANAGEMENT SYSTEM 153
- 8.4   CONTROLLING.........................155
- 8.5   REPORTING 156
- 8.6   SELLING THE COMPANY AS AN EXIT STRATEGY............................157
- 8.7   THE NAKED TRUTH: AN EXAMPLE OF SELLING A COMPANY...................160
- 8.8   PRACTICAL PART: COMPANY MANAGEMENT 165
- 8.9   IN BRIEF: COMPANY MANAGEMENT 166

CONCLUSION..............................167
IN SALES YOU NEED TO GET "NAKED" 167
AM I A SALES PROPHET IN MY HOMETOWN?...169

THE CURTAIN OF HISTORY

When Jesus had finished these parables, he moved on from there. Coming to his hometown, he began teaching the people in their synagogue, and they were amazed. "Where did this man get this wisdom and these miraculous powers?" they asked. "Isn't this the carpenter's son? Isn't his mother's name Mary, and aren't his brothers James, Joseph, Simon and Judas? Aren't all his sisters with us? Where then did this man get all these things?" And they took offence at him. But Jesus said to them, "A prophet is not without honour except in his own town and in his own home." And he did not do many miracles there because of their lack of faith.
(Matthew 13:53-58)

FOREWORD

Dear Reader!

In front of you is a book with a special title and just as meaningful content. Sales are presented through aspects that are necessary for the development of a successful modern company. In these times of the so-called "Get it done" generation, the "Naked sales" book questions traditional sales methods and attempts to reveal the key elements that are necessary for a company's progress.

This book is written as a practical guide and therefore focuses on entirely practical performance that every business and salesperson needs in their everyday lives. In addition to direct sales, it also focuses on segments which you as a businessperson should perform every day, as it attempts to present sales as the practical final execution of a company's business processes.

This book will take you from personal sales motivation through to sales basics and up to the final step of selling a company. Since the book focuses on practice, each chapter finishes with practical assignments and a "cheat" sheet, i.e. a summary which you can use in your sales.

There are quite a few theoretical "sales" terms in this book which remain undefined as the book focuses on implementing those in practice; they are mentioned so that you can give them extra attention if you are interested in sales theory.
Such words and other emphasised terms are written

in italics. It should be noted that the book itself is written in a "naked" sense, and thus does not focus on wordiness. Its aim is to evoke the practical sales goal in the reader, which is to "sell". When explaining sales theory, the author tries to present his experiences in the first person. But when he wishes to emphasise the practical part he turns to You directly.

The book is full of practical examples from the everyday world of sales. They are marked with "The naked truth" to further reiterate the idea of execution.
With a big dose of humour, this book will not leave you indifferent and will lead you into the world of entrepreneurial and sales action while, at the same time, increasing your knowledge to even better develop your company.

Dominik Božič

INTRODUCTION

In front of you is a book about life. A book about the life of a salesperson, a book about a life of selling and progress in general. When achieving our goals we almost always use selling methods or different sales approaches. For example: when courting a future partner (remember? sold), negotiating with parents (almost always sold), with your children, colleagues, subordinates in your company, with members in a society, at an interview for a new job. In our lives, we are always selling something - without realising it.
The problem occurs when we want to consciously sell something. We usually stumble when selling becomes our obligation.

The only rule I stuck to when writing this book was: "Don't over-complicate and wander into theory." This resulted in a practical guide for a salesperson's every day needs. It doesn't matter if you're an experienced and sly businessperson, a complete beginner, an expert in a technical field, an artist or just an everyday person - you alone will have to test the message and the usefulness of the tools presented in this book. Everything I wrote in this book, I have tested in practice. In the real world. The many mistakes I have made on my business journey and the correctional activities to fix these mistakes have encouraged me to share my experiences with others. If, when reading this book, you see the outline of a situation that you haven't yet experienced in practice, and the information you gained thereby provides you with a preventative measure, my mission for writing this book will have been completed.

The key question asked by future businesspeople is when to begin their business journey. Different periods in time and different political situations are more or less favourable to entrepreneurship. This was true in the past and modern trends show this to be true also in the future.

Opinion on private entrepreneurship in Slovenia after 1945 is full of stereotypes. More often than not the conversation on entrepreneurs began like this: "He had fallen out with everybody in the company so he decided to become an entrepreneur or craftsman." The tone is scornful and humiliating. Of course, not all stories are the same. As sources can attest, entrepreneurs had to obtain consent from the communist party to allow them to become craftsmen.

Different rules applied to different sectors. In socialist times it was quite normal to be a craftsman if you were a shoemaker, but after 1985 it was not so common for a craftsman to have a large construction company. Of course, many things changed, especially after 1991. Unfortunately many companies closed down as well (which was not common in socialist times) as demand on the domestic (Yugoslavian) market was greater than supply.

In the time of tax reliefs (at the end of the 1980s and the beginning of the 1990s), craftsmen's children had an advantage in opening a company because their parents had established businesses and a desire to open a company on behalf of their children due to generous tax reliefs.
This was also the time when I started my business – a time when entrepreneurs did not have to pay tax on profits for the first year. I have to admit this helped me a lot, as I would have struggled to pay it - my beginnings were the same as everyone else's, hard and

made up of small steps.

In the late 1980s, entrepreneurship more often than not began with undeclared "afternoon work" by workers otherwise permanently employed in public companies. All they needed was to have a little business sense and satisfactory or quality products or services. A craftsman did not require initial capital, so their company grew slowly and, after each new job performed, they were able to purchase the additional tools required for their solutions. More complex manufacturing activities were most often started by Slovenes who worked in other countries. They invested their savings into the complex manufacturing activities they had discovered while working abroad.

When talking to the pioneers of those times, entrepreneurial jargon and the use of terms such as business vision, goal setting, strategic planning for achieving goals, business plan, financial plan etc., were not used. Their highest values were hard work, integrity, persistence and stubbornness. Even if they never told the stories of their beginnings or explained the milestones in their business careers, all the "natural" steps in a company's evolution had occurred. Some occurred sooner and some later. And some never occurred due to a lack of professional knowledge and skills that were not crucial for the existence of the company at that time. The result of this was the company ceasing to grow and successfully develop.

Some parents like to boast about how young (some even as young as 18) their children were when they embarked on an entrepreneurial career. However, the start of a person's entrepreneurial story is not limited by age. If you have a great entrepreneurial idea when you are 15, then that's the right time to start. The same is true if you are 99 years old. An individual's business sense is mature when knowledge, capital and other abilities required suffice. This is when you should embark on your entrepreneurial path. This is the right moment. In the current "information revolution" times, the age of the idea holder or the executing team is irrelevant. It's a well-known fact that the computer world is best managed by the youngest members of our society, whose knowledge from a directed education does not limit personal fantasy or goals set.

The main trend and aim in modern entrepreneurship is thus to develop solutions up to a point when they can be sold as quickly as possible. To meet this goal, modern tools and methods, which are presented later on in this book, are necessary.

But now, it's your turn.

What will you do to become an entrepreneur who takes advantage of a given opportunity and achieves success through their talent and sales tools?

1. SETTING GOALS

Determining what we want in life is becoming increasingly demanding in the modern world. We live in affluence, but are aggressively attacked by marketing messages and adverts. We find it difficult to recognise ourselves and our true wishes and needs. Our consumer society is heavily indebted, but most people have too many assets. Including those they don't need.

It's a good idea to stop and think for a moment. Are we unable to communicate with ourselves well enough to automatically, i.e. intuitively, recognise our true desires and needs? Such awareness is achieved by only some people - but don't be afraid, there are quite a few methods which can help you determine your talents, skills and knowledge. By knowing such methods you will be able to undertake any activity you desire and have a talent for. A combination of both is key to a successful professional career.

1.1 WISHES AND ACTIVITIES

Psychologists use professional methods whereby they, as we can often hear, "take us back" to our childhood. It is always a good idea to search for the point at which your wishes and the activities that realise these wishes parted ways. If this sentence doesn't resonate with you, this doesn't mean

that you lead a completely passive and uncreative life; instead, it means you are one of those people who renounced or adapted their wishes due to various personal and environmental limitations. People who do not do this in a business sense can usually be deemed "a success".

Aren't we ourselves one big speciality - a project which no one has yet fulfilled?
To help yourself with your key question, you need to analyse your knowledge, skills and talents.
First, answer this question: "Why do we do what we do?" This way your awareness of the wishes-activities relationship will become much clearer. This awareness is key to your personal and business success.

1.2 ACHIEVING GOALS

The most general or lazy answer to this question is, of course: because of human needs. In theory we could list a number of them, but let's focus on six key needs. There are four basic human needs (security, affiliation, significance, connection) and two emotional or spiritual needs (growth and contribution).
You can truly explore this topic at seminars titled: "How to set goals" (and other similar gatherings with similar meaningful titles).
You'll be surprised to see how much you can achieve on your own, using a simple method, and will learn how great your potential is in your own definitions of knowledge, skills and talents.

1.3 TALENTS, KNOWLEDGE AND SKILLS

Proverbially speaking talent is needed to achieve high goals. The first idea you have to master in the art of correctly setting goals, is the fact that you yourself are the talent. According to scientists, every person has talent. Many never explore it in their lives or, better said, never find it. This refers to an impulsive or instinctive reaction by an individual or their adaptation to a certain situation.

It is interesting to note that talent can't be transferred to another person by learning. Talent defines us. It is therefore important to build your business career in accordance with your talent.

The term skills covers many different areas. A skill is the ability to carry out an activity in a certain area without any mistakes, and to repeat it several times flawlessly. Unlike talent, skills can be transferred, i.e. we can teach them to others. It is a fact that skills cannot replace talent, but it's true that we can perform them more easily if we have talent for them. Hard work and training are the most guaranteed path to excel at skills.

Knowledge is an area which is clearly understood by everyone. Knowledge is usually obtained from our parents, in school, at university, seminars and such. Experience is an important part of the area of knowledge. We acquire experience by ourselves through activities and work. Results are created when we combine knowledge and skills with activities. Unfortunately, there are also many cases

when people with knowledge and skills fail to fulfil their potential, due to objective or subjective circumstances, and thus fail to create something good for themselves and others.

1.4 PRACTICAL PART: DISCOVER YOUR TALENTS

Those of us in the coaching business are aware that people never find enough motivation, time and courage to deal with the topic of knowledge, skills and talents themselves. This is why I will present a few simple tools you can use on your own or together with your partner or friends. You will learn about a field which studies abilities and sheds light on everyone's personal abilities.

Task 1: *Skills and talents I already have or have already mastered*

On a piece of paper write down twenty skills that you have mastered. For example: I'm excellent at driving a car, I find it easy to connect with people, I can easily talk in front of a large crowd etc.

After you've listed twenty skills, a few days later work on them so more and add some more. In doing so you will learn about your potential.

I once heard a story about a man who had made some poor life choices and business decisions and ended up bankrupt. These problems led to him experiencing insomnia.

Since he could not sleep, he found a job as a taxi driver and only drove the taxi at night. He learned about his skills by coincidence, regained his income and was able to provide for his family again. Later on he opened a taxi company, where he still works today. It's amazing how much knowledge and life-skills he acquired. He experienced the depth of the world through the eyes of a man in the centre of events - from riches to rags. Later on he opened several companies and is now a successful businessman.

If you want to achieve a sufficient level of realising your abilities, you need to know the skills you've mastered and their opposites; i.e. the skills you have not mastered, but would like to.

Task 2: *Skills I have not mastered, but would like to*

On a new piece of paper or in a table write down

twenty skills you would like to develop. For example: playing the piano, programming computer software, playing golf etc.

To increase your motivation, I will tell you about my experience of wishes and talents - I often use this example if my clients ask me about my own discovering of talents. Particularly at the beginning, sport was one of the key activities in my life, but I liked other things as well, such as music. For my thirty-third birthday, I invited my family over for dinner. My wife's parents gave me an acoustic guitar as a present. I accepted their gift with enthusiasm, but at the same time felt uncomfortable as I didn't know how to play the guitar. This then became a personal challenge as well as a chance to prove myself in front of other family members. I thus started to develop

a skill which I had not mastered. First, I tried to learn to play the guitar via video lessons, but this did not lead to the desired results. Since my wish was more powerful than failure, I started taking guitar lessons. I usually practised in my office late at night, before going home. Of course, I will never become an amazing guitarist, but I learned to play well enough that I can play at our company's parties. I am, therefore, proof that it is never too late to make your wishes come true and to develop skills we haven't yet mastered.

Task 3: *My knowledge and education*

This task, which will lead you directly to establishing what it is you want in life, is again a list of your special knowledge and education. Ask yourself, can you teach others how to fix a car and can you fix cars? Do you excel at accounting?

If you're a mechanical engineer whose hobby is cooking

and wine-making, you can create a "paradox" out of your talents by having more awards and recognition in the field of your hobbies than in the field defined by your education and the one you professionally participate in daily. There are many examples of people succeeding in an area they love doing and turning it into a successful business story.

Your hobby used to be a cost, and it ends up a source of income for you and your family. This can't happen without suitable circumstances. Something must go very wrong in the primary line of business - most often this means losing your job - which in turn leads to pursuing your hobby

professionally, i.e. focus on the area in which you already possess talent and skills. It is hard to decide on a private business career while being in the so-called "comfort zone" since we are aware that starting is never easy. What prevents us from doing this is fear.
If you're capable of self-motivation by looking to the future and you enjoy thinking of the results you will achieve, I urge you to decide on a private business career at once.
As is clear from what you have read so far, life balance is something that needs working on.

Write a list of knowledge and education you've obtained. Include all education, training, certificates and the like. Write down your hobbies in a second column. Try to connect them or try to see if any of them coincide.

Task 4: *Special knowledge and skills I wish to learn*

It is important to allow yourself to dream. Usually, our biggest hurdle is excessive realistic thinking and thereby fear, which pulls us back each day. You have to become aware of the fact that it's never too late to

Setting Goals

return to books or to learn about something which may be unusual for where you live or for your age. Many people I meet are worried about other people's opinions.

"What will people say?" Visitors to my lectures are always shocked at my direct answer to this stereotypical question (which is asked too often). I usually make it stand out even more by exclaiming: "Screw them!" People who like dealing with others, are too afraid to see their own reality and don't have the guts to learn their talents and to try to develop new skills. No one is more important to your happiness and progress than yourself. Why, then, should you worry about others?

In a new table, write down twenty areas of knowledge and skills you really want to learn.

Task 5: *A list of people I know*

Never forget about the people you know and who are important for your development. Don't forget about your schoolmates from primary or secondary school, nor your ex-colleagues and friends. This list will help you find the potential you have in your friends.

Experienced entrepreneurs know that they don't know everything on their own. Doctor Ernesto Sirolli named three things that are essential for entrepreneurship: sales, production and accounting. He also added that a person who could master each of these areas to perfection has not yet been born. This is why it's important to find a wider circle of people you know - it will enable you to find a partner to develop your business idea.

As an interesting fact, let me mention that the famous billionaire and visionary Sir Richard Branson never mentions the word ME in the first pages of his biography. He only uses US, which means that he built his Virgin company with his friends.

You can also mark on your list those people who have already succeeded in the endeavour which you are planning.

Task 6: *A list of role models and mentors*

A list of role models and mentors will help you to learn from other people's examples. This will make it easier for you to walk a path already trodden by others, even though you might not experience that directly.

You can meet up with your business friends and colleagues at mastermind evenings where you can present your ideas, ask questions, get suggestions or even find a partner for your project's execution.

As the practical part of this task you can organise an evening to present your ideas. Invite those people who are, in your opinion, experts in the areas in question and can help you with questions or comments. Invite them by explaining the purpose of the evening. Explain to them in an informed manner why you respect them and their opinion. This way you will experience interesting and instructive evenings while getting the chance to connect with others and co-create a culture of business development in your community. Just remember - it doesn't matter at which level or in which entrepreneurial cycle you are in at any given moment. What matters, is where you would like to get.
Your role models can help you, especially during periods when things don't go smoothly.

On a piece of paper or in a table write down your role models and the reasons why you look up to them.

Setting Goals 17

Task 7: *A list of people I wish to meet*

When performing this task, make sure you're not too unrealistic, i.e. listing people who are too far removed from your world or you don't know personally, or even those who are no longer with us. This task is about finding mentors of similar values and defined paths that make sense for you.
Just think how many Elvis Presley impersonators there are. Many live from their work as his impersonators.

Don't let anyone ridicule or even humiliate you because of your daring thinking. If there are such people in your surroundings, replace them or don't discuss your views with them. People who pull us back and don't respect our views of the world are not suitable company for people who wish to work, are ready to accept responsibility for their actions and live their lives according to their wishes and not according to someone else's norms.

Write down a list of people you wish to meet. Also, think about how they could help you.

Task 8: *I liked doing some things when I was younger*

One of the most important things on your road to completely fulfilling your potential and knowing yourself is to think about your childhood: "What were the things I used to like to do when I was younger?" You can talk to your parents about this.
For example, what did you use to say you'd like to become when you grew up? Children are dreamy, indirect and honest. That's why the Scouts have a merit and skills collection. Those are obtained by helping a friend, working with the elderly, hiking and similar activities. The motivational purpose of the praised achievements is exceptional. A person who has achieved

a goal gets praised for it; this way, they can never say: "I'm not good at anything, I'm rubbish."

Write down your past achievements in a table. With the help of carefree deliberation on your current life position, you can learn what your dream job could be. I'm certain that you should not leave out this task. In addition to your achievements also write down the things you liked doing when you were little. Check if any of your achievements were also your childhood wishes.

Task 9: *Imagine you won the lottery*

For the "harsh realists" this may be the most difficult task. Imagine that you won an exceptionally large amount of money. Your task is to close your eyes and daydream. Later on, write down all the things you would buy or spend the money on. Make your dream list. Remember: If it's written down, it can come true.

For a technical view of this idea, we could say:
"You need a plan to make a good product." This is why lottery winners often end up in trouble; because they don't have a plan of what to do with the money. Think about it: lots of money can bring about huge expenses. For example: you buy a large yacht; the mooring costs are EUR 20,000 per year and on top of that you have the insurance costs and other expenses.

If you don't have a regular income and you have already spent all your winnings, you're spending more than you have.

Several years of experience with people from both sides of the classroom, the student and the lecturer, have taught me that only one part is missing from the list above - the part which some people find very difficult to do. The part in question is conclusion or completing the given tasks that will bring you to the finish line.

Task 10: *A promise that will burden and motivate you in the future*

Write down a promise that will motivate as well as burden you in the future.
It's important to make a promise to yourself and to write it down. A promise of dreams, wishes, hope and everything you wish to come true hereafter. The list should include goals which you'll achieve through your actions in the future.

1.5 IN BRIEF: SETTING GOALS

Every goal contains:
1. A clear picture of what is being achieved.
2. A measurable value.
3. A date to achieve the goal by - realistic and partially pressed.
4. A list of activities to be repeated daily that will bring us to the goal. Repeat them for at least 3 weeks so that they become a habit.
5. Daydreaming and enjoying the final goal as if you had already succeeded.

Correct goal setting is one of the most important things for achieving our goal. But all this is useless if you don't implement this plan correctly. In the next chapter you will learn how to implement goal setting in a business sense and how to achieve those goals.

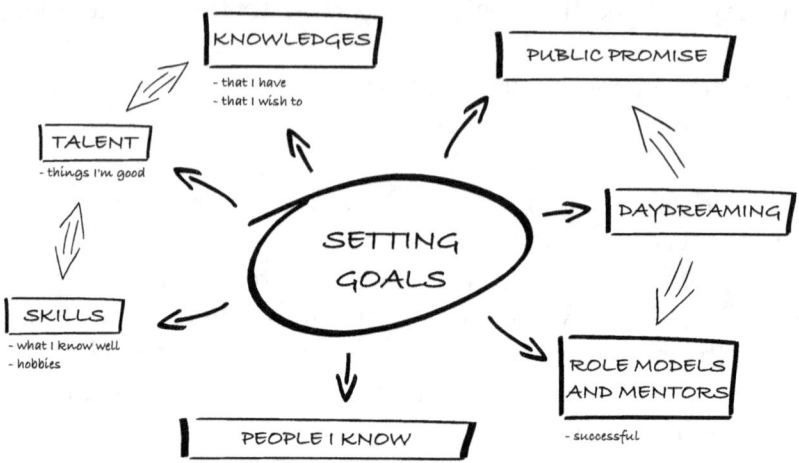

Mind map 1: Setting goals

2. THE BASICS OF SALES

Understanding the needs of potential buyers is the basis for successful sales in the future. We buy things because it makes us happy. Shopping releases certain chemical reactions in our brains that are connected with feeling good. Take buying a piece of clothing, it improves our self-image in society. Think about it. If someone notices your new piece of clothing, you see it as a valuable social event. Whether you admit it or not. It's essentially a sense of power which lifts us above ourselves. A person who likes other people and likes to help them has the perfect foundation to become a successful salesperson. The skill called sales entails detecting a need and finding the right user – a buyer for your solution or product. I personally think liking people is the basis of a good salesperson. We often meet salespeople who are condescending and egocentric. Such people cannot be successful in the long run since they don't feel empathy and thereby don't recognise people's needs. Sales is also one of the basic business functions of a company giving sense to entrepreneurship. What is produced must be sold. This is how crucial income for the development and existence of a company and the people (and their families) who make up the company is generated. Sales is not a trick or a scam - it's a noble ability which is not self-evident even in cases of pioneering discoveries in a certain area or innovations that change human lives for the better.

2.1 SALES IS HELPING

As mentioned before, a salesperson must, first and foremost, like people. They should perceive sales as a way of helping people and not as a source of profit. Profit is a logical consequence of helping the customer. Believe me, everyone who you've really helped will gladly pay for what you are selling. If you realise that your solution will not help the customer, withdraw from the sale, as it won't bring you any long-term benefits.

2.2 PRODUCT OR SOLUTION

A solution is something that helps people reach their goal and can be sold as a service or as a product. It can be a technological, medical or other solution developed with the purpose of helping the buyer. Salespeople almost always strive to meet a buyer's needs, whether they are life, technical or psychological needs. A product is a consequence of a solution or, better said, something "tangible" representing this solution. The word "solution" represents a wider notion of a company's mission; this means, it represents much more than just the logical consequence of the company's production, i.e. the product. Later on you will learn how to distinguish between, use and internalise both notions.

What do you sell?

What do you sell? Most salespeople sell products. A buyer wishes to solve or resolve a certain challenge or problem, and therefore they need a solution. A solution that will solve their problem partially or completely. A solution can be a product, a service or a combination of the two. Never underestimate the extent of the buyer's problem since you don't know how big the challenge really is.

For example: Buying a luxury car can be a collector's solution or one that helps the ego or cures a complex. Such purchases are usually defined as prestigious. Even prestigious purchases are solutions to a certain problem.

What really is a product?
Some parts of your solutions have to be worked on in modules within your company, which means that you produce a product. A salesperson should always look for the customer's problem and try to solve it. We are looking for the customer's so-called "pain", for which they need a solution. Our solution is thus a product developed for this purpose. This is why we sell the customer a solution that can be developed with our know-how and by using the product. A product is thus a traditional product, but also one that is usually accompanied by a solution, i.e. our knowledge, which gives added value to the product.
Everyone knows what a product is, but in the sense of selling this term is often used incorrectly - this is demonstrated in not meeting your sales goals.

Why is the term product so unacceptable?

The term product is unacceptable since your customer can search for a similar product on the market and compare it to yours. Such comparisons don't bring any benefits to either you or the buyer.
More often than not, the mistake of offering products and the damage connected with this is reflected in the forced reduction of sales prices or providing discounts. This is a consequence of customers' expectations and their not recognising the value of your product due to the abundance of similar products.
It therefore often happens that a customer finds us and requests our product. The customer requests our product without first providing any information about what kind of challenge the solution is needed for. This

kind of sales conversation usually results in a very low price for the product that the customer automatically connected with the solution.

It therefore often happens that the product is not suitable for the task at hand, which leads the customer to believe that our product, and thereby our solution, is no good.

A good example of poor customer decisions in a purchase where the salesperson is co-responsible for the poor decisions made by the customer, is the purchase of "amateur" equipment intended for professional activities.

In the next example, you will learn about the difference between the product and the solution.

The naked truth: An example of selling solutions

A gardener who uses his lawnmower daily for his work (e.g. 8 hours per day) buys a lawnmower usually bought by homeowners and not by professional gardeners.

The average homeowner with a garden cuts the grass once a week or every two weeks. This means that the lawnmower of the entrepreneur in question will have experienced an annual load in the first half of a week. Its lifetime will be much shorter than, for example, in my case. We can thus conclude that after the stoppages, time for servicing and poorer quality of the service are added, the entrepreneur is almost forced to use professional tools that will lead to profits. This means a similar product and its use can mean two different sales solutions.

Selling a solution is a response to the customer's problem or challenge. This doesn't mean custom made solutions are always required; the customer's problem can be resolved through our already developed products and methodology.

Starbucks coffee shops, well-known all around the world (2500 locations worldwide), are always located in excellent locations. Their central offer to customers is an instant indication that they've reached the agreed place. While travelling around Italy in the 1980s, Howard Schultz, former marketing director at Starbucks, got the idea of "teaching" Americans how to drink espresso. The owners of the company rejected his idea. This led him to start his own company and later buy the Starbucks brand, whose business philosophy, in addition to selling excellent coffee, is also a well-recognised company logo, great location, free internet access etc.

Does Starbucks sell coffee? Yes, but this is not the only solution offered. A meeting place and lifestyle branding are the added values. The branding is of course set as an Italian café with a variety of coffees served, but prepared in an American style. Which means fast. What's crucial is the fact that while waiting for the person you've arranged to meet, you can read your e-mail, eat a croissant or buy a takeaway coffee. As is true for every other big chain, its operation is based on various life scenarios and trying to meet as many needs as possible. Of course, Starbucks will not burden you with how long you've been sitting there or how much you've eaten - they receive their part of the payment from the value of the coffee you drank while being there.
The mission you wish to achieve is an important advantage that you have to be aware of. Many people may offer a product, but your solution is unique. Regardless of the fact that your coffee shop is one of the ten coffee shops in the same street, yours is a solution to something special. In the example above, Starbucks wishes to bring the culture of drinking coffee closer to people all around the world and accommodate local culture - this is what makes it a global and successful company. Therefore, we can say that your mission is

the driving principle of your solution. The solution can be modified and adapted to your customers, but the mission of your solution is rarely changed and is thus your company's main constant.

2.3 MISSION

The mission of your company, business idea or solution is one of the most important principles and one that has to be nurtured and continuously renewed. The mission is what dictates development and, at the same time, adapts your solutions and products to your customers. The mission usually isn't connected to profit or the economic side of your company - it usually has a "higher" goal. Very successful companies set high-flying goals, which have a direct impact on the company, as their mission. Such operations bring large profits, but they aren't the priority. Facebook, a well-known company, serves as a good example; it's goal was never to become the most valuable social network; instead it aimed to provide digital connectivity to people all around the world. A well-defined mission can always help us when experiencing financial difficulties since it reminds us why we opted for the concrete solution, product or business idea.

2.4 SALESPERSON

Who or what is a salesperson?
By definition, a salesperson is someone who buys with the intention of reselling. They cover the costs of sales, marketing and labour with a profit, the so-called profit margin. You can find such definitions in various pieces of professional literature, which haven't changed much throughout the history of sales. Such definitions, though, can also do a lot of harm to salespeople and sales in general, since they can be misunderstood and negatively perceived by laypeople (not salespeople),

even though they make a living from the goods or services sold.

A good salesperson is an advisor. They are amicable people with a desire to help. If they make a mistake, they usually lose their customers' long-term trust, which they worked very hard for. That's why salespeople are careful and compliant - even though stereotypes describe them as the complete opposite. Remember, arrogance and an excessive desire for earnings aren't characteristics of a true salesperson, since only a foolish salesperson would ruin their reputation by acting irresponsibly. What a "real" salesperson should be like is revealed later on.

Preparation for a meeting

It is much easier to prepare for a business meeting after you've understood the necessary facts outlined earlier in this book. When you are well-aware of how you can help your potential buyers, always make sure you prepare on the basis of concrete ideas and situations.
Some believe preparing for a meeting is connected with a catalogue, a price list, a suitable outfit and not being late for the meeting. All of these are important, but they usually won't help you directly convince your buyers to buy your solution. When in a meeting, you will exchange ideas, impress each other and suggest collaboration, resolve issues etc. Many things will happen. That's why you need to prepare thoroughly. The time needed for preparing will, of course, shorten as you gain more experience, but in order to avoid unsuccessful meetings, you should prepare for the meeting more thoroughly than by just choosing the right outfit and arriving on time. Most importantly, you should know what type of meeting it is and should prepare accordingly. You should make a clear distinction between a meeting focused on discussing

ideas or increasing trust or just a work meeting when the main sales phase is already behind you. In addition to setting goals, good preparation also includes well-selected words. Write down the words you are going to use. These are the questions that will lead you to the next step of the meeting.

People often use a sympathetic preparation method, usually summarised using indents. For example: first I'll say this and then I'll ask that. Although this framework of understanding might be important, it is not necessarily very useful. Such a list is suitable for experienced salespeople, but definitely not for beginners or people who wish to enrich their business communication knowledge by using sales tools. It is essential that you write down or learn the exact sentences you will say in a meeting. For example: "Dear Mr. or Mrs. X, people usually trust me to..." You must repeat the words that follow several times to ensure that your preparation is sufficient. The main goal is a successful meeting - regardless of the sales stage you are at.

First impressions

The first rule of being a successful salesperson is looking presentable. Never forget that sales, and thereby business, are created by people. Everyday we use intuition, non-verbal communication, our senses and past experiences. So, when we meet a new person for the first time, we automatically make use of all these options to create an assessment of the person standing before us. First impressions often don't reflect reality, but are subconsciously stored in our memory and play an important part in continued communication.

Which are the things that a customer will notice/see in a salesperson? A clean face, hair, clothing and shoes. This is followed by clean hands, nails and the tidiness of the outfit. As the proverb teaches us, "clothes make the man," and how to adapt your clothing to your work environment is not only a big question but also a necessity you must be aware of. Every work place demands a different outfit. A salesperson in a sports shop, a saleswoman in a cosmetics department, a sales representative, an insurance representative. Every place of work or area has its peculiarities, and clothing adapted to them is required for more successful sales. In the so-called first sales addresses the salesperson represents a role model for the buyers, since they want to become more like him/her and buy a product or a solution from him/her. A well-arranged combination of shoes, trousers and shirts on the shelves and also on the salesperson's body is essential for making a sale, even if it is subconscious. A salesperson is a company's ambassador, representing the culture and message of the company. The salesperson's appearance represents control over the product and thereby security and trust for customers, and this usually leads to a successful sale.

The next speciality is smell, which people perceive very differently. The worst possible experience is the smell of sweat - especially when we haven't showered in a few days. There are also people who have serious problems with this; if you're one of them and your job includes communicating directly with people, you should consider seeing a doctor. Bad habits can also affect our appearance. If you are addicted to any of them, the person you're speaking to will have a difficult time maintaining a suitable level of communication.
The smell of cigarettes or alcohol is perceived by some as the most off-putting factor in a possible collaboration. If you smoke, make sure you finished your cigarette at least ten minutes before the next conversation - and not by flicking the stub on the ground before entering a potential customer's office. Even smokers find a strong stench of cigarettes disturbing, since no smoking is allowed in public places.

Some salespeople also have certain eating habits that can seem very "disrespectful" to partners in business communication. Garlic and onion are, of course, the "most popular" tools to put off potential clients. We mustn't forget canned fish, salamis, pâtés etc. And animal lovers often forget to "keep" the smell of their beloved pets at home.

Good manners and etiquette, which are considered coincidental or not the most important in modern companies, particularly in new age "start-up" companies, are still an important factor in making a first impression. The business etiquette expected at a meeting of course depends on the differences in cultures and the type of company. Salespeople should be able to adapt to their potential customers' habits so that they don't waste time and energy on something that is not particularly useful. Our purpose is to satisfy the need presented by the customer. Don't forget - a satisfied customer is the best investment you can make in your own marketing and your company's marketing.

Of course, there's nothing wrong with the above habits and bad habits - I don't believe I have the right to judge people's personal habits, but I would like to point out the possible unintentional mistakes that could damage your path to success. Your appearance and behaviour are not all that matters for suitable conduct in front of your client – what's more important is how you speak and, thereby, "how" you sell.

Preparation for a sales pitch

When preparing for a sales pitch, salespeople usually focus on the text they will use when meeting a new, potential customer.

Similarly to what I said regarding preparing for a meeting, what we should focus on is the words that we will use. It's very important that a salesperson knows when to take a step back, so that a potential customer doesn't feel pressured into buying their solution. That's why the sentence "think about this solution, take all the time you need" is considered "blasphemous" by some. Even I wouldn't use it if I didn't have full control over the sales process and didn't know that the interlocutor is a suitable potential customer who has a problem and is aware of the consequences if the problem isn't resolved in time. You should know that some sentences, which are not always suitable according to sales theory, needn't be problematic in practice depending on the given situation. A sales pitch also consists of improvisation, meaning that you are able to listen to your customers and ask them such questions that will bring you to the final solution and result in a win-win situation.

Well-known experts in the field of presentation and sales take a long time to prepare for their presentations. Apple's Steve Jobs was known as one of the most attentive speech preparers. He would spend 170 hours or more selecting the sentences and movements that he used in his presentations. In my work, I meet salespeople who have been successful at their work for many years. Their speeches are almost always the same or slightly adapted to the current customer. They are the result of many years of experience. All they usually need is to refresh their knowledge a little and change any bad habits acquired over the many years of selling.

I often ask salespeople if they know how to sing. I'm referring to a technique used by singers that is useful for learning how to speak "from the stomach" and not "from the throat". If a six-foot sixteen-stone professional opened his mouth and sounded like a whistle or a chicken, it would have a highly negative effect. Speaking from the throat is common and is what we're used to. Professional speakers are aware that their work is not finished in one day, but takes several consecutive and tiresome days. The same is true for salespeople. We participate in many meetings and talks, which is why we need to look after our voices. Preparing your voice is the first step - the next step is saying enough with few words. Learning how to speak "from the stomach" isn't easy and I suggest you seek professional help from someone who has mastered it. In addition to the above, physical fitness is also important. Our bodies get exhausted by the pressures of intense thinking, presentations and public appearances; this is reflected in the quality of your public speaking and, in the long-term, your well-being.

The naked truth: An example of a sales pitch

Salespeople are often worried that they're not prepared enough for meeting a concrete customer, especially if it's a big customer; luckily, the desire to overcome a great challenge is usually greater than the fear (which is best overcome by being well-prepared for a sales pitch).

I remember the first meeting I had with, now, one of my best business friends. I had come to a production company with a noticeable exceptional dynamics of business events. The owner and director was stretched between procurement, quality control, shipping etc. As would any proud entrepreneur, he first showed me the production area of the company. While doing so, he was answering the phone, reprimanded a colleague etc. In short, I witnessed intense chaos, which for him meant his normal working process. Once the tour was over, we sat down to talk about the technological equipment he was going to invest in. Even though I had, by that point, quite a bit of experience in business communication, this situation was very challenging. The director hardly listened to me and replied in the same way to almost all my questions. While I was driving to my next customer, I had enough time to think about how I should approach this project. I was driven by a great desire to close this deal since it would be very beneficial to our company at that time. Therefore, I was facing two challenges. The first was the fact that our solution could really help this potential client, and the second was our company's financial situation. My main mission and wish influenced my decision to approach this project with my trump card. At the end of the meeting, I agreed to prepare a solution for the client that we would discuss at the next scheduled meeting. Of course, the client said that there was no need for a meeting since they would like to examine the quote first and then make their decision. I knew I wasn't the cheapest provider. But I was certain that our solution offered the best quality, and was supported by an exceptional team that could carry out the project.

I invested a lot of time and effort preparing for the next meeting. I spent a great deal of energy analysing the director and his assistant to establish who the real decision maker was. The decision wasn't difficult; technology and economics are both very important topics in any company. But on the basis of the events which unfolded when I visited the company, I decided it was the director I needed to impress. I could see he had a strong character and wouldn't tolerate an indecisive, long-winded speech. I left home very early for the next meeting. As it took me three hours to get to the company, I left home at two in the morning and got to the company at five in the morning. I was certain that the director would also be there at this time. He welcomed me and asked me if I was crazy arriving so early.

I replied: "Forgive me for arriving a bit earlier than we'd agreed, but at our previous meeting I noticed that a very intense atmosphere is created here after seven in the morning, and I would find it very difficult to disturb you then as you seem very busy."

He offered me coffee and we sat down in his large office on the first floor. I introduced myself again in two minutes and then asked him questions to establish their actual need; after that, I presented my solution. I suggested he examine our solution together with the technical team and proposed a date for visiting a reference installation, a few hours' drive from their factory. The deal was done. My determination and preparation had convinced the like-minded client to buy the solution.

You should never forget: the owner's and director's personal values are often the biggest motivation for big purchases or big business decisions. Always stick to the following rule. Integrity, high quality and belief in the team behind you will make your promises come true.

Sales pitch in brief

Ask yourself:
How long have I prepared for my pitch?
Have I written down the key sentences I would use to persuade the buyer?
Have I prepared the key negotiating conclusions?
What are the buyer's personal values and the values of the company they represent?

Also take into account the following six principles:

  a) Physical fitness
  b) Suitable clothing in which you feel confident
  c) Detailed "sales vademecum" you will use in the meeting
  d) A well thought-out timeline for the meeting, presentation and conclusions
  e) Excellent voice training
  f) Lots of exercise - words

Possible complications

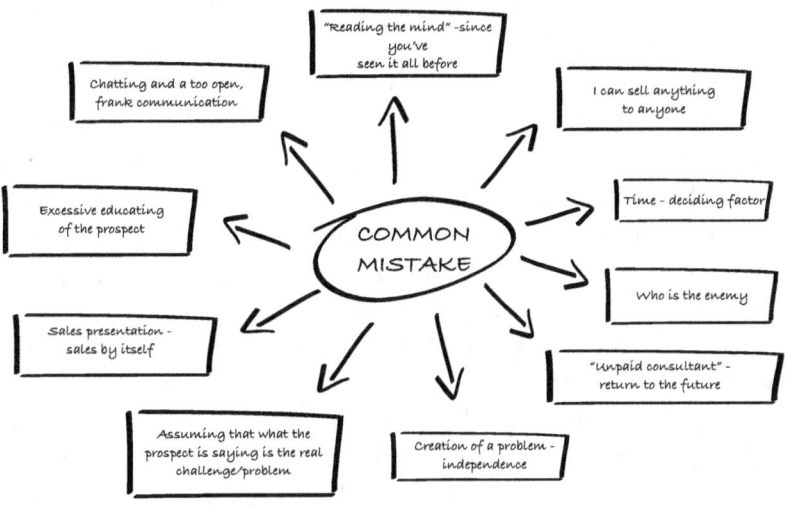

Mind map 2: Common mistakes

Although we prepare thoroughly for a sales pitch, complications often arise. It's important not to try and avoid complications, but to try and control them.

More often than not, a complication arises when we are unable to define who the final decision-maker in the current sales situation is. The salesperson completes the first meeting, which we will call "intelligent communication" as it means that the verification and the potential client's needs have already been identified. When we're in a meeting with a potential client and wish to successfully close the sale, we need to establish if there is anyone else in that company who might be interested in our final solution. Purchasing officers or heads of technical departments, heads of HR and heads of other departments who are looking for a solution to their challenges always name their managing director as the decision-maker since they are the one that signs the order.

The goal of every successful salesperson is thus to get a meeting with the managing director in order to

present their solution to them. Often this depends on the size and the purchasing value of the project and on the size of the company. If your solution exceeds the sales decisions of the employees, and meeting the managing director is essential (which is, of course, a good thing for the salesperson), a crucial mistake or a so-called sales complication can occur. When you meet the managing director at the second or third meeting, it often happens that it is the first meeting all over again, i.e. establishing needs, and not the meeting to close the deal as many salespeople might think. You should take into account that heads of departments and the managing director don't have the same problems. The managing director has hired the head of the department to resolve their problem. If the head of the department is also a businessperson in the wider sense of the word, they are able to present the need for a solution to the managing director in the right way. If they aren't skilled at that, they can also pose a risk to the entire project and if you use the wrong evaluation or approach you won't be able to sell your solution.
The advice I give to all my clients is not to compromise a sale by deciding that the head of the department is the main, leading professional, i.e. the decision-maker. That is why it is important that you start the meeting again by asking the right questions to establish the needs. After the managing director realises that they need a solution in the area you've discussed, you continue by saying: "Your colleague mentioned to me..."

Wrong! You should not, of course, say this sentence. This common mistake leads to "bruising" the managing director's ego. It will feel like a direct attack on the managing director's integrity, and they will, in most cases, react by rejecting your solution. If you succeed in leading the meeting as described, the managing director will feel like the person who came up with the proposal and the solution. Of course, you'll immediately think that this is immoral or that you don't want to work with such a company. If that's your thinking, try reversing the roles. Don't forget - selling means mainly adapting to the purpose of meeting the buyer's demands within your financial capabilities, and is one of the basic virtues of the Naked sales method.

Often, complications at meetings can arise because of your past. If you weren't at fault for a complication with a customer in the past, and if that happened due to the policy of the company where you were employed, you should be honest about it and tell your potential buyers at the start. Don't judge others, be honest and earn a second chance. Facial expressions will usually warn you that something is bothering the person you're talking to. That's when you should talk openly and explain that you have no bad intentions, but wish to provide sales advice as best you can. Reactions will vary, but you will keep 80 percent of your potential clients if you have good knowledge of what you're offering.

Complications at meetings often arise from national, racial and political diversity. I recommend you stay classy and don't comment on politics and similar topics, even though you may think it would make you more likeable to a potential customer. As mentioned before, you need to understand that successful entrepreneurs will appreciate your integrity and the ability to complete a project that will benefit their company.

The naked truth: An example of a sales complication

If you have only just started a company, you have to start at the beginning. This means your meetings cannot be pretentious and you have to be aware of your inexperience. My first meeting with one of the most renowned managing directors finished as soon as it had begun. It lasted for about twenty minutes, but merely due to the politeness of the gentleman I was trying to sell my solution to. Through a friend, a highly respected businessperson, I got the opportunity for a meeting at the very top of an esteemed international company. I arranged the date and the time of the meeting through the general director's secretary. To this day I remember entering his office, which was covered in glass mirrors, stone pillars and stretched out to a roof terrace covered with a lawn of the greenest grass. All elements of power - intended to make visitors realise how "small" they were in comparison. But I was completely confused by the person I was there to meet - the exact opposite of his surroundings. Elegant, polite and friendly in words and in gestures.

I'm not sure what - my youthful exuberance, excessive confidence or perhaps unmatched naivety - blinded me to such an extent that I arrived at the meeting completely unprepared. When I recollect this meeting today, I think the situation resembled stepping out in front of a client and saying: "Have you, perhaps, thought about me? Is there a chance that I could do something for you?" You would probably say: "What an idiot!" Exactly. I failed to redeem my joker and arrived at that meeting like a bull in a china shop.

A mistake salespeople often make is that they themselves don't know why a buyer should buy their solution, and due to their sloppy presentation the buyer is unable to recognise the advantages which could convince them to enter into collaboration.

Salesperson in practice

A salesperson is someone with an open character, who adores human communication. The salesperson's life mission is to help their customers achieve an easier, more pleasant life. A salesperson is not a deceiver or a person who would misuse their customers' trust.

In addition to their values, a salesperson is also defined by their knowledge. In theory and in practice. This book focuses mainly on the latter.

Theory and practice

Sales theory was created from a simple impulse to help other salespeople be successful. This means that sales theory developed from the practical sales of a successful individual. Later on, some philosophers developed the sales theory further by making assumptions and hypotheses. There's nothing wrong with this, but the so-called "naked sales" method is based on the principle of testing theory in practice. After that, the sales process must be upgraded by experiences obtained through practice. Once a project is successfully completed, we then attempt to "turn" this experience into theory so that we can transfer it to other cases.

Improvisation

Improvisation represents an important part of sales, particularly in the sense of sales communication. The buyer should not, or shouldn't be able to, recognise the moment when a professional approach is supplemented with or replaced by improvisation. Improvisation is one of the key virtues of "naked sales", but I should point out that this is "trained" and "learned" improvisation based on preceding theoretical knowledge and experiences.
When working with clients I often see great micro field experts collapsing before their meetings, and the knowledge, which they do indeed master, evaporating due to their stage-fright.
A recipe you can stick to when the need to improvise arises, is the following:

1. What kind of problems are arising in the environment I am in?
2. What possible solutions could my clients make use of?
3. Why is my solution the best solution?

When you mention each of the above points, you can explain the issue in a few sentences; but don't forget the next point and the direction you've selected to successfully complete the sales meeting. A quote by Jerry Barber, the famous golfer, is apt here: "The more I practice, the luckier I get." In our case, this means that only a "well-trained" salesperson is able to improvise at such a high level that the client or buyer would never notice it. Of course, we can't do without luck in similar cases, but it's true that it's not really luck if you have plenty of it. It's luck if you don't need it.

You can train your ability to improvise well, since every thorough preparation reduces the risk of failure. You'll learn this later on in the book.

The salesperson in everyday life

A common untruth spread by non-salespeople is that salespeople are always selling. Perhaps that's true, but we're not selling the solution, product or service that we market for our livelihoods or, better said, our businesses. In their everyday lives, salespeople usually wish to create new opportunities for their business lives by talking, "networking" and expanding their contacts. Some salespeople don't get that and can become quite aggressive and annoying to those around them.

A recipe for the good life of a salesperson

A recipe for the good life of a salesperson is similar to that for pancakes. If you follow it, everyone is happy - your family, friends and your business partners. I suggest you stick to the following:

- Manage your time - plan your business and personal activities with the same degree of commitment (e.g. seeing your son perform at

nursery).
- Supplement your knowledge and focus on your current business; plan and visualise your path for the next ten years.
- Don't indulge in needless education - don't study something which is currently fashionable or might be good for your business. Such thinking is a waste of your energy.
- Hire external experts for areas you aren't good at or those which take up too much of your time.
- Spend your free time and social activities with highly motivated people who have set clearly defined goals and are in a settled relationship. Salespeople spend a lot of time on the road, which means they get along well with a partner who is equally dynamically involved in their lives. You will be a better salesperson and entrepreneur if your partner shares your views.

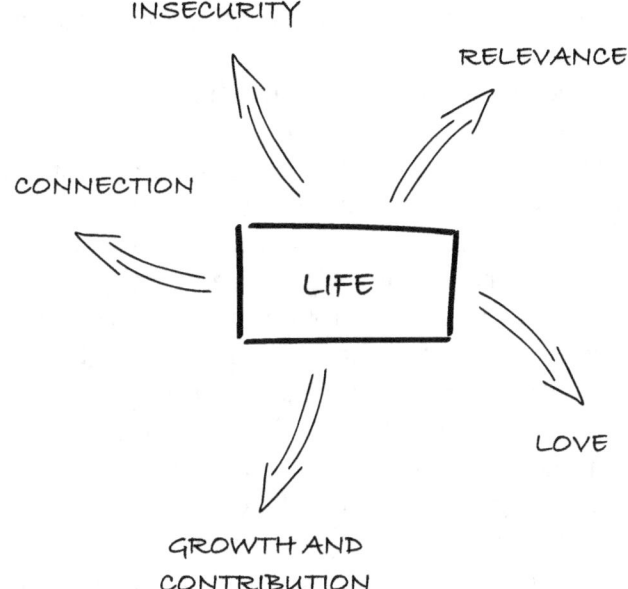

Mind map 3: Life

The salesperson and family

Poor time management is the most common mistake us salespeople make regarding our private lives. This means that we often don't distinguish between time for work and time for family and hobbies.
We often only realise this when our relationships are already damaged and it's unfortunately too late to fix that.
Time management workshops are an excellent tool to help you develop the philosophy behind your time.
But, these things are so specific that it is impossible to describe or understand them in theory. Many experts around the world who don't have children give advice to parents as to how to raise their children. And it's the same in this case. I believe family is an important value for a salesperson and serves first and foremost as motivation and a source of drive in moments when things don't turn out as planned. Good salespeople are advisers who solve their customers' problems or tackle their challenges. This means they are only human and sometimes need help. Of course, they can use all the sales knowledge and methods for themselves, but often they are prevented from doing so by their own ego. It is important to understand and distinguish quality time, similarly to when focusing on a client or sales project. When you're with your family and when you're selling. This refers to the skill of managing your time, and the task is anything but easy. In particular, those sales or businesspeople who come from smaller markets or smaller companies are not the best at separating work from family. For them, the life of a business or salesperson is not a job - it's a lifestyle. Despite this, you should bring the quality of your life to a level that makes your life worth living. What I wish to emphasise, is that we all get caught up in temptation, mainly because we don't think enough about ourselves and our work. That's when we start believing that we should do

anything it takes for our business. At least at the start to get things going. Suddenly, twenty years have gone by and we blame our nervous actions and frequent failures on others. And, what is most unacceptable, we blame those we love the most.

Habits and bad habits

Despite the fact that we all want to ensure a better future for ourselves, our families and especially our children, in the sense of opportunities and commodities, it often happens that we forget to distinguish between good and bad habits. In this sense, the biggest enemy in the life of a modern salesperson or businessperson is the mobile phone. Even though it is one of the best inventions for a successful business, it can greatly disturb those around us and lead to many unsatisfied faces, quarrels or unsuccessful meetings. The indiscreet use of modern digital devices will soon replace the bad habits that were once considered the salesperson's biggest annoyances. Another stereotypical bad habit is "showing-off", in the sense of living beyond one's means. Even if this is done in good faith and with the aim of obtaining more renowned customers, this kind of behaviour more often than not ends up in disaster. More traditional annoyances, such as food, alcohol and the smell of cigarettes are still very present in the sales community. Often, salespeople forget that their appearance and their behaviour do not only represent themselves but also the company's solution and, thereby, the company for which they're selling as well. Younger salespeople often look up to young "star" entrepreneurs and think that the only thing that matters is what they say, and not how they present themselves or what they're wearing. T-shirts and jeans are one such bad habit. You have to understand that you won't always be selling to IT companies that usually tolerate such clothing. I stick to the rule that a salesperson can never be overdressed. You will never be rejected on account of looking too good.

Another bad habit that many entrepreneurs can't stand is being late. You know yourself that this bad habit is difficult to break. Even though it might sound bizarre, punctuality at meetings will come with experience. You should understand that arriving at meetings too early can disturb and show a disregard for a company's rhythm. As we are being flooded with mobile phones and other smart devices, so-called micro-rules are appearing that dictate how to use them for successful business communication. Not picking up or returning phone calls are two main bad habits that indicate a salesperson or a company in general is not a serious business partner. I strongly recommend avoiding this in order to build a solid business integrity. The next in the series of "unserious" bad habits are unrealistic promises. They will severely reduce your credibility, perhaps even to the extent of affecting your future business dealings. Never forget: for you, the best reference is a recommendation by a fellow entrepreneur. Strictly avoid the double bluff and forwarding information to the competition. Such behaviour will not only prevent further collaboration with your business partner, but is also a criminal offence in most cases. Even if you think this can't happen to you, you might reveal something of crucial importance for your business partner when you're trying to win over a new client in good faith.

Some of the more grotesque bad habits are also excessive entertaining, drinking and being intimate with business partners while on business trips. I advise against such behaviour since it will, among other things, distract your focus from doing business and bring about mostly negative consequences. Salespeople's bad habits don't differ much from those of people from other business areas - they only demand common sense. The same is true for the recommended habits.

As mentioned earlier, be a thorough, but not a too early salesperson. Don't come to a meeting more than five minutes early. Dress according to your target group. Always promise only what you and your team can deliver. Don't forget that the client comes first and that they always like to hear praise. Keep your mobile phone on silent during meetings and never, under no circumstances, browse social networks. In addition, pay attention to the time spent during a meeting, as you don't want to take up too much of your customer's time. Remember, good solutions are simple and not much time is needed to explain them. Yes, those solutions sell well.

2.5 THE SALESPERSON'S TALENTS, KNOWLEDGE AND SKILLS

Figuring out what we really want in life is an eternal question. The easiest thing to do is to define material goals. Emotions are much more complicated. That's when we ask ourselves if we really feel well, if this is what we've been looking for and similar questions. As we've established before, each of us has a talent for something. In some cases, this can be clear from afar. As I mentioned before, I believe that if you don't like people, you shouldn't work with them. If you're a people hater, every effort you invest will feel like "hell". Think about a waiter's job. Someone who loves their work can serve twenty guests in a very short time, as well as laugh, find time for small talk and you still won't be left feeling like you've been waiting too long. Such a person has a talent for their work and for working with people. The opposite is someone who works slowly, whines, is unfriendly etc. Technically, they might be equally good, but what separates them is the talent - in this case a social sense and attitude to work. Yes, those are talents as well. The same is true for traditional sales.

Tools for recognising the salesperson's talent

The tools for recognising personal talents that could be useful for the wider public are described in Chapter I. Everyone can recognise themselves in the methods mentioned. The difference is in cultures, focuses and social conditions. You know the saying: "A healthy person has a thousand wishes, a sick person only one." The similar is true in discovering personal talents. A large number of opportunities can often blur our vision. Or, someone else's thinking can influence our own decision.

Parents are no exception in influencing their children's decisions. We gave our children life, but we don't own their lives. Our task is to help them discover their talents and help them become independent. It's not their fault if we wrap them in cotton wool until they're thirty and later on realise that they're unable to work or provide for themselves. And you know very well who criticises their children the most if they're still living with their parents when they're thirty. Those who spoiled them - or taught them so.

The key existential question in recognising talent is, is it better to catch fish so that our children can eat, or is it better to teach our children how to fish. You would probably say:
"Of course, we need to teach them." But due to our modern lifestyles and lack of time we can quickly end up in a situation where we say to our child: "Leave it, I'll do it more quickly."

Talents don't manifest themselves only in the simple things we do every day, but also in changes when adapting to our surroundings and our lifestyles.

As mentioned, the key information most of us want to obtain in the different periods of our lives is to find out what it is we want.

The same goes for recognising a salesperson's talents. To discover a salesperson's talents, we need to answer the questions from Chapter I - of course, in a selling sense.

A talented salesperson primarily has a good sense for establishing the needs of a potential buyer:

- is a good listener,
- asks the right questions,
- on the basis of their findings, says exactly what the buyer wishes to hear / buy,
- knows exactly when to step back,
- likes helping people,
- isn't pushy.

What am I good at as a salesperson

To establish what you're best at as a salesperson and what you need to improve further in order to increase the number of successfully closed deals, try to answer the following questions:

- Are you selling something you're genuinely interested in?
- Is your vision poorly set?
- Do you give up too quickly?
- Do you think your solution is so good that you would buy it?
- Does your solution resolve your client's problem?

2.6 TYPES OF SALESPEOPLE

There are several types of salespeople. In addition, there are many different classifications, but I like to divide them more practically, the so-called "naked" way.

Essentially, there are only two types of salespeople. Salespeople and non-salespeople or successful and unsuccessful salespeople.

If we develop this statement further, we can divide salespeople according to their inclinations, principles and activities. There are prepared and unprepared salespeople. Admittedly, there are no statistics that would show us which type is more successful. You could say that even preparation isn't as crucial as the salesperson's mission or desire to succeed and make a living. Next, you can see a table with salespeople's and non-salespeople's characteristics.

Successful salesperson	Unsuccessful salesperson
pleasant	pushy
prepared	unprepared
scheming	over-confident
stands behind the quality of their solution	with a price complex
cheerful, full-of-life	depressed, generally unsatisfied
interesting	boring
brief	time stealer
stands behind their promises	lacking integrity
self-confident	with no self-respect
respectful	vulgar
good listener	does not listen
adaptable	overly-uptight
self-critical	takes offence
professional attitude	doesn't know how to keep a professional distance

Stereotypes

It is interesting to see how very alive the stereotype of the salesperson who will "trick us" and sell us something we don't need is, even in professional sales. As a customer, you have to be aware of your weakness, that sometimes you are seduced by some products and unconsciously and without thinking about the consequences decide to buy them. Of course, the salesperson is not to blame; instead, this is a consequence of your personal wishes and of the product's effective marketing. As is common in the "normal" world, we often rely upon stereotypes in the sales world as well. Here, there are quite a few. Being aware of stereotypes can also help you to better define yourself and to, thereby, improve the quality of your sales method.

In practice, a salesperson can be:

- Calm and prudent - carefully planning sales closing, as that is of key importance.
- An exceptional professional adviser - clients who need professional help buy from them despite perhaps not having the best sales techniques.
- Pushy and annoying.
- Perverse and insulting.
- Vehement and with a high opinion of themselves.
- Insecure and not sure of their product - the deal is usually closed out of sympathy.

2.7 DEVELOPING THE SALESPERSON'S STRATEGIES

Wise men claim knowledge is never enough. But nothing would have ever been created if we had always waited for this knowledge to touch us.

When entrepreneurship comes from the heart, it is easy to know when is the right time to begin. If you're embarking on this path purely because of money and your mind is on other things and not on the benefits for your buyers, it could happen that you'll run out of steam on this difficult mission. The right time is when you're feeling strong enough and your plan B is to return to your employment career level. Embarking on a path that you don't fully "feel" and later on finding out that there was a suitable opportunity, but you failed to grab it, means making the biggest mistake of your life.

It is necessary to make an overview of goals and devise a strategy for achieving them. Come up with all the possibilities that are currently available to you. If you can afford an external adviser or coach to guide your brainstorming in the right direction, you should do so.

There are four types of sales strategies depending on the goal:

- Goal oriented - you wish to be the first, the best, you wish to make a certain amount of money and get approval from your colleagues or managing director.
- Customer satisfaction oriented - in it for the long haul. A strategy that doesn't bring immediate results, but is a safe investment.
- Enjoying your work - seeing work as fun. A modern and increasingly popular approach. Eventually, it might become the only one suitable for modern entrepreneurship.

- Performance of your career.

The strategies are usually intertwined and there's no clear dividing line between them. With coaching it is possible to determine the types of salespeople and thereby their sales strategies, and to build a good sales team.
The same goes for ordinary people. A successful work team can be created using an analysis of the types and strategies. Usually we have to determine everyone's wishes and goals. What is key, is that everyone realises where they see themselves in life further down the line. With this in mind they can continue their business life and try to achieve the common goals of all the participating members. With such awareness you'll be able to define the strategies needed for a successful salesperson or sales team.
Of course, a good strategy doesn't encompass only the company's mission. Developing the sales strategy must coincide with the reality of the solution, meaning it must be economically justified.

If a client is, for example, interested in sailing boats and their company is located at 800 metres above sea level and 200 kilometres from the nearest coast, the true salesperson cannot accept the sales strategy as it is evident that the client's customers are located elsewhere.

Sales strategies are continuously changing. What is important, is that they also develop. They develop on the basis of goals or the salesperson's intention. The next four suggestions will help you develop the strategies outlined:

- Goals: Develop your strategy on the basis of your personal wishes, as you will achieve or even exceed it in the end. Develop this strategy

by writing down your intentions every day. This way you will develop your strategy in every detail.
- Satisfied customers: Think in the following way: "My salary and money are the result of satisfied customers; I love my customers, respect them, resolve their problems for them and fulfil their wishes."
- You enjoy talking to people.
- Constantly work on your sales techniques, since you need to realise that the current step is necessary for the next step in your career. Fight, fight, fight, set boundaries and then fight, fight, fight.

Direction taken from the lives of real people and colleagues should serve as the priority when preparing your strategy. It is crucial that you check the goal you have set on the market. You need to establish who your buyers and the users of your solutions are.

2.8 SALESPEOPLE'S MOTIVATION

As I emphasised before, salespeople are people first and foremost, and the same is true for their motivation. Motivational techniques in sales differ slightly from general ones since a non-motivated salesperson can do more damage to the company than a shop floor worker. Even though I was once called a motivational coach on television, I have to admit that I'm only a passionate salesperson who genuinely, as I have already and will stress again in this book, likes people. And this is the original part of motivation itself.

The Basics of Sales

Mind map 4: Salesperson's motivation

A sales team can be easily motivated using the following methods:

- Organise regular sales-motivational meetings for your sales team.
- Train your salespeople, since knowing the solution and sales techniques will make them more confident.
- Use sales tools and invest in them to provide your sales team with the tools to sell more.
- Adapt motivational speeches to individuals.
- Don't forget about rewarding your sales team and the structure of doing so.
- • Set personal goals with your salespeople according to the procedures described in Chapter I.
- Don't forget to give praise.

Salespeople's self-motivation

Jokingly, we could say that a company is as strong as is its weakest salesperson. Be aware that motivational techniques are only a guidance as to how to trigger self-motivation in a salesperson.

Self-motivation is key to success. It can be strengthened with the following:

- Set a material goal - money, car, house, holiday home, boat, watch, travelling.
- Set a precise date by when you wish to achieve this.
- Determine how much you need to sell per day, week, and month to meet this goal.
- Determine which activities you need to do on a daily basis in order to meet this goal. For example: 60 calls, 3 meetings, 1 contract etc.
- Enjoy thinking about what it will be like when you will have done this.

Just remember, setting goals is the fundamental self-motivation technique. In this case, it's concrete goals. It is much easier to achieve goals if they're tangible. Similarly, you can transfer such tangible goals to your company's wider goals and thus help realise your company's mission.

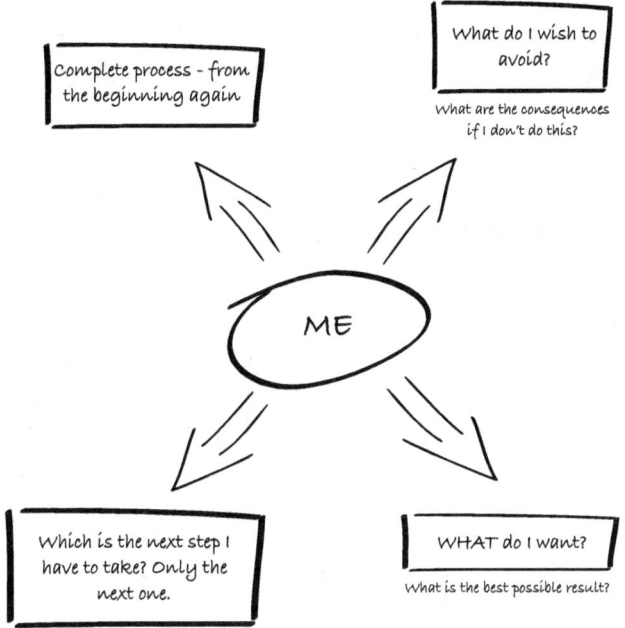

Mind map 5: Me

Motivating others

As a good sales adviser or entrepreneur you have to motivate other team members in addition to your sales team, since they co-create your solution and thereby your company. Use the following to help you do that:

- Motivation using monetary rewards - a weekly or monthly bonus; it's best if all team members receive it, not just an individual. If an individual isn't working in the right direction, other team members will either motivate them or reject them.
- Motivation using promotion - younger team members wish to prove themselves to become team leaders or decision-makers.
- Measuring and publishing results on notice boards - to highlight the best ones and thereby

encourage natural competitiveness.
- Motivation with individual awards - additional training abroad, participation in workshops, events.

2.9 STORYTELLING - THE BASIS OF A GOOD SALESPERSON

A successful salesperson expands their experiences, no matter what they sell. That's why we often think of a successful salesperson as a storyteller. The advantage of sales is the fact that there is a person on each side of the business event. People are curious and inquisitive - that's why we like stories. Some might make fun of this, but they still like to hear a good story. If you disagree, think of a joke that your colleague told you last week. Yes, it was just a funny story.

Storytelling ignites feelings in people that enable them to identify themselves with the solution being sold. If you wish to become a good storyteller, try to take note of the following:

- Each story contains:
  - fear and weakness,
  - an event or suspense,
  - a lesson or good feeling.
- A good story should include provocation in the form of pain experienced by potential buyers.
- Through the story explain the realistic possible solutions by using previous clients as examples, but be careful not to reveal too much.
- Favour your solution and provide reasons for that.
- The story should always involve values that the potential client expresses through non-verbal communication; for example, if they are wearing sailing shoes, you should ideally tell

them a story connected with the sea.

2.10 THE NAKED TRUTH: EXAMPLES OF STORYTELLING IN A GIVEN SALES SITUATION

As I mentioned earlier, non-verbal communication is an important part of preparing for storytelling in a given sales situation. As the basis for concrete examples of storytelling we can also include:

- Commend the product, hardware and office design.
- Listen to the managing director's stories.
- The story's ending should include your solution.
- In your story, first sum up what is good, and also hinge on the general good - in a similar way that fables do.
- Elaborate on the problem to increase your listeners' awareness that there is a problem.
- While storytelling, identify the possible solutions.
- Explain the details of the best solution - usually your solution.

2.11 IMPORTANT SALESPERSON'S SKILLS - TEN RULES

People often interpret a good salesperson as someone with a knack for selling. Unfortunately, no one has yet discovered the gene for that knack. Personally, I think the skills possessed by a successful salesperson can be learned. But, it's also true that virtues, such as kindness and a desire to help people, are very difficult, if not impossible, to learn. Some people make important findings spontaneously and almost without realising.

Read about the following ten skills, and you will discover that some of them come completely naturally to you.

1. Detection - the wrong evaluation of a potential client who will never become a buyer.
2. Trust - building trust is important if you want your customer to tell you their business secrets. Start building trust from the first moment you meet. Share your knowledge about their business and show that you care.
3. Presentation - practice, practice, practice ... get rid of all the hesitations (um, ah, but etc.) and make sure it's brief, simple and efficient.
4. Listening - you have two ears and one mouth. Make sure your sales communication observes this ratio. You can only find out what the customer needs if you listen to them.
5. Story - emotions create logic. A suitable story for a concrete customer has to be excellent and make the customer excited. Good storytellers have the advantage here.
6. Objections - the ability to manage comments is one that separates successful salespeople from unsuccessful ones. Think of the reservations the customer might have in advance, and react to them with an informed reply including your solution. Controlling tension is a central part of this talent, since you do not want tense communication with your clients.
7. Sales closing - implement the sales process in small steps and finish it when you get the final "Yes" from your customer.
8. Recommendations - are the best tool for making your business "boom". Salespeople often don't dare to ask for a reference. Show your buyers that you value their opinion and recommendation. When you've successfully

completed a project, you simply won't be denied a reference.
9. Relationship - giving up is something that everyone in sales comes across at one point or another. You will achieve victories by repetition. Keep working, rejection is just a lesson and a motivation - it is not a failure
10. Writing - a clear message is invaluable. Reading and writing are necessary daily to strengthen our abilities.

2.12 PRACTICAL PART: THE SALESPERSON IN PRACTICE

Task 1: *List all the benefits or advantages that the end user of your product or service will gain.*

Task 2: *Think about how many times buyers purchase your solution/service in a given period of time.*

Task 3: *What should your appearance be like to suit the customer?*

Task 4: *Think about why the buyer should buy your product/service.*

Task 5: *Choose a product. In a few sentences, describe why you sell it.*

Task 6: *Where should you buy a vacuum cleaner, in a shop or from a sales agent?*

Task 7: Pre-preparation for a meeting.

Task 8: Think of a solution. Try to sell it to friends as know-how.

Task 9: Convince a colleague not to drink alcohol at a party.

Task 10: Get yourself into an awkward situation at a party.

Task 11: Write down the talents that you have and could use in sales.

Task 12: Write down what type of a salesperson you and your colleagues are.

Task 13: Write down how you will motivate your sales team.

Task 14: Transform the motivational script for your sales team so that is self-motivational and present it.

Task 15: Storytelling. Weave your product's presentation into a story and present it.

2.13 IN BRIEF: THE BASICS OF SALES

1. Sales is helping. Love you customers and help them.
2. Sell solutions and not just products.
3. Always keep your mission in mind when doing business.
4. Try to be a salesperson without bad habits, think of your appearance and make sure you make a good first impression.
5. Carefully choose the words for your sales pitch.
6. Learn to "improvise".
7. Ensure efficient time management. Plan your business and private activities with the same degree of commitment.
8. To be a successful salesperson, you need to be aware of your talents and skills and make the best of them.
9. Motivate your sales team.
10. Motivate yourself.
11. As a salesperson learn to be good at storytelling.

3. SALES TOOLS

In the previous chapter you learned about the basics of sales and what a salesperson should be like in order to increase their yield on sales. You also learned about the basic rules of conduct dictated by practice. Sales tools are tools that supplement a salesperson's knowledge and them as a whole. With the help of such tools, a salesperson controls the sales cycle to ensure nothing is left to chance. There are theoretical and practical sales tools. As usual, we will focus on the latter. But we cannot ignore the theory in this case since it is very helpful - the main purpose of theorising the sales tools is to help us transfer the successful methods to other methods we use in sales.

3.1 DEVELOPMENT OF A BUSINESS IDEA THE REQUIRED KNOWLEDGE OF EVERY SALESPERSON

A good salesperson must know how to develop a business idea since this is the only way they can understand it fully and then sell it. A business idea should not only be a good idea on its own, but it should also be feasible - meaning that it can be sold.

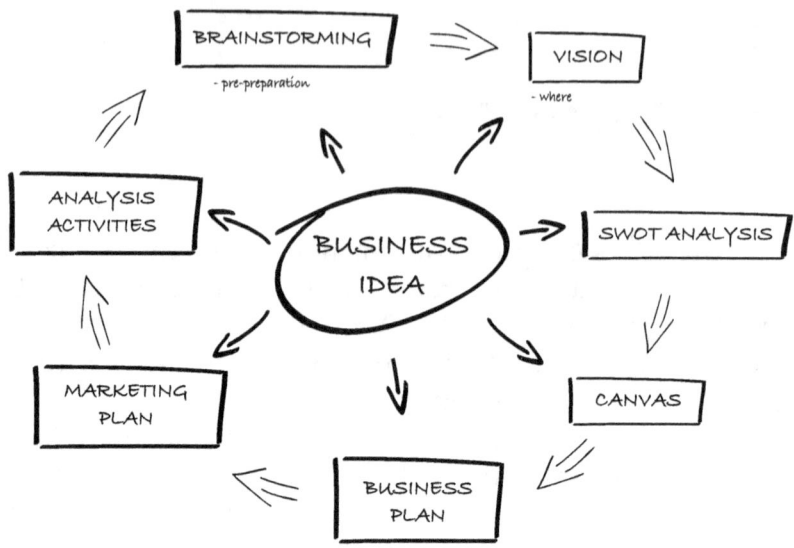

Mind map 6: Business idea

Practical tool for developing a business idea

Practical tools for developing a business idea are in abundance, but according to the "naked sales" principle, you should derive it "from yourself". If you do, you will think of the best ideas that you'll also be able to sell using your sales knowledge and tools.

Tools for developing a business idea

As already mentioned, there are many tools for developing a business idea. Let's not forget, a business idea is at the same time also your company's mission and vision, which means that it might serve as your only incentive to keep going when things get tough.

- Brainstorming: Pre-preparation, i.e. brainstorming, is the most important part of developing a business idea. We can distinguish between product or solution brainstorming,

where the aim is to find out how to develop a solution in the form of a product or service, and sales brainstorming used for determining who would even need or buy our solution/product.
- Vision: As a tool, our vision guides us through our idea - showing us where we're headed and what changes our solution will make in people's lives. It is a key tool that has to be conceptualised in a way that allows only minor changes. If the vision can't be defined in the long-term, there's a big chance the success of your idea will also not be long-term.
- SWOT analysis: For this purpose you should prepare a SWOT analysis where the threats serve as the right opportunity for finding the right solutions. SWOT analysis is a very popular sales tool used to quickly determine the four elements of your company: strengths, weaknesses, opportunities and threats. Since lots of information about SWOT analyses is already freely available, we won't go into detail in this book. But we can say that all the weaknesses and threats have to be neutralised, i.e. we have to be prepared for them, to ensure the long-term success of our company.
- Business plan and canvas: A business plan is a tool that has almost always been used for obtaining financial means from more conservative institutions, such as banks. For their own needs or the needs of the company, modern entrepreneurs usually make a canvas or a similar presentation instead of a business plan.
- Marketing plan: As a step to the realisation of our business plan, we often prepare a marketing plan, which is extremely important for a successful launch on the market,

especially when we haven't yet sold anything and our advertising funds are limited. A marketing plan is thus essential as it will ensure that people hear about you.
- Activity analysis: To carry out an activity analysis, you should follow the next three steps (especially at the start): brainstorming, activities and analysis. First, think about who the hell would even buy your solution and how. In the second step, specify a particular time period - not too long and not too short. A month is just right. During this period carry out the planned activities that you came up with during the brainstorming. It is very important to know how many calls were made, how many meetings were held and how many sales were closed. The last step is an analysis, which will pave the way for your future business operations.

During the analysis you can ask yourself many practical questions, answers to which are key for further business success. I talk about concrete questions for the analysis tools in the section dedicated to just that.

The biggest mistake salespeople make when developing a business idea is assuming why people buy from them and what kind of people they are.
Such mistakes can be minimised or even eliminated with the right procedures and analysis tools.

When you've obtained real information about your business operations using the analysis, you can design your sales steps:

- Step 1: Where are your potential buyers and how will they find out about your solution?
- Step 2: How will you determine that they're

- really your potential buyers?
- Step 3: An intelligent conversation where you ask yourself the same questions as potential buyers would ask themselves -Why the fuck should I listen to you?
- Step 4: Determining the needs of the concrete buyer or their pain, which is the reason for deciding to buy your solution.
- Step 5: Presentation of solutions that are a logical answer to the mentioned pains.
- Step 6: Closing the sales – there are no sales without closing.
- Step 7: Additional sales activities expanding the existing buyer's extent of purchase.

I should point out that additional sales tools can be used in all the sales steps. In the intelligent step this is the so-called sales vademecum - i.e. the central presentational solution or a pitch that convinces the person to whom you're talking to enter into a collaboration with you. It should answer all the possible questions the buyer might have and the reasons for them.

Naked truth: An example of using tools to develop a business idea

Provide a short answer to each question:

- I IMAGINE
  What will I be selling?
  Who will be buying this?
  What will my buyers gain with my product?

- WHAT WILL I GAIN
  What will my sales price be?
  With which payment methods will the buyers pay me? How else could I make profit with this business?

- I'LL MAKE MYSELF SEEN
  How/where will buyers find out about my offer?
  What will I do to get my buyers to recommend me to others?

- SUCCESS
  The business will be a success when I achieve the following results:
  Number of buyers: _____ or annual income in the amount of: _____

- CHALLENGES, OBSTACLES
  Possible special difficulty (challenge 1)
  Proposed solution for challenge 1

A good idea no one wants to buy is just a good idea

Remember, there are many good ideas, but people won't pay a thing for such incomprehensive ideas. There are many business ideas. Think about it, I'm sure you have one every day. One that would bring you millions. But... An idea is only as good as its execution. If you don't realise it, it's the same as if you'd never had it.

3.2 ENTREPRENEURIAL STAGES

Every company's business operations and development consists of so-called entrepreneurial stages. You can imagine them as periods in a company's life. People go through childhood, puberty, active years etc. in their everyday lives and a company goes through different stages in its life-cycle.
They go something like this:

- Period 1: Start-up or beginning.
- Period 2: Market integration and increased recognition.
- Period 3: Existing customers expect something

new. Development and competition emerge in response to your sales activities.
- Period 4: Reinforcing the trademark.
- Period 5: Changing of generations or selling the company

Knowing the entrepreneurial stages is very important since it is easier to direct your step to the next, realistic period if you know at which stage you currently are. This, of course, means good, organic growth of your company. Not being aware of or not taking into account the entrepreneurial stages can lead good, financially sound companies to ruin. A good example of this are start-ups from Silicon Valley which, despite their substantial financial backing and good business ideas, don't find a place in the market in the long-term.

Pitfalls of entrepreneurial stages

The company's growth depends on the vision and strategy of the mastermind or the team. There are cases when the expansion of success is caused by the market or, better said, high demand. The market's demand for modern and technologically advanced solutions that facilitate some modern daily tasks can overwhelm the entrepreneurial knowledge and potential of the company that is developing them. There are quite a few mistakes or pitfalls that we must avoid in our company's stages.

- **Excessive initial success**
Imagine a teenager who has suddenly become a TV star. To his manager and sponsors he is just a tool for increasing their profits, and overnight he's achieved something he couldn't have dreamt of. That's when the teenager experiences a mental collapse - age appropriate and suitable for his mental development. Very few manage to get through this period without any consequences. The lucky ones have a good mentor

or guardian by their sides.
- **Expanding the company too soon**

In the same way as is true for a start-up, expansion or enrichment as a result of a few good sales moves or a good product that happens too soon can harm the company since its management isn't able to carry out the activities demanded by it.
- **Unsuccessful market integration**

It often happens that we did everything right, but the company hasn't settled on the market. You should know - luck is also needed for rapid market integration. If the integration isn't going as planned, you should go back to brainstorming and analysis tools, and try to remove the main obstacle that is preventing the integration.
- **Competition**

It often happens that the company management "rests on its laurels" and fails to move with the times. That's when the competition takes over the company's market position. Usually this happens because a company's owners don't know how to hand over the management of the company to younger successors who know the answers to the current market demands.
- **Selling the company**

Often, a successful company goes out of business due to not being sold This means that the owners decided against selling it even though the management hadn't found a successor as they don't wish to sell "their baby". Such companies are usually put out of business by the pressures of the competition or the market itself. The pitfalls of entrepreneurial stages are very common and can be managed by making the right decisions based on the sales tools. Remember, things work differently in a highly focused activity where development and vision are more important than simply accumulating profit and where organic growth isn't limited by time. Such a company deals with the following question: "Do we wish to become the global number one in our field or do we want to make millions?" Practice shows that the

Sales Tools 71

latter is a consequence of the former, but not vice-versa.
- **Vision**

The first option - "becoming the global number one" - is very clear and team members know exactly which of them is a specialist in a particular area in the company. In this case any conflicts that could lead to failure are very rare. Most often conflicts arise from team members' different views and opinions, but these also serve as a driving force behind "becoming the global number one" since they promote progress and the development of innovative ideas. In the second case, when the company's primary goal is to make millions in profit, failure doesn't occur when partners or colleagues disagree; it happened long before that. Usually, it is the result of human greed and participants looking out for their personal interests. This is human nature and it doesn't happen in a particular period of the company's development. Some of the responsibility for this often lies with their life partners, who provide negative encouragement. Unfortunately, there are too many stories like this.

- **Fragmentation and jack-of-all trades**

Even if you start out being self-employed, it's a good idea to write down which steps are needed for your company to function well. It often happens that you have too much work on your hands and you end up doing the things you're not qualified to do. Your tasks throughout the day are those of production, if selling - sales, if you also compose sales agreements you perform the tasks of the administrative and legal departments, and when paying the bills you're the accountant. When you plan the company's vision and protocols, and its investments, you're doing the job of company management. The more precisely you specify tasks and processes and assign them to different business functions, the easier it will be later on when you entrust tasks to new employees. At the early stage of a company's development, the management position is usually neglected since a technical or production expert doesn't have any managerial skills. It doesn't matter though, you can learn everything you need to learn.

- **Ego**

Once you've learned how to delegate, you can eventually become the biggest "clog" in your company's development. If you want to avoid this, you have to experience a change of thinking, meaning that you need to delegate tasks and then control, like a manager, their implementation and progress. Problems often arise when a company's "pioneers" don't allow their colleagues to carry out certain tasks, even though they would be better at them. Here, we're dealing with the ego. Naturally, the entrepreneur's ego should be quite big since with it comes great confidence, which is crucial for beginning your life as an entrepreneur. Controlling your ego isn't easy; to avoid the ego trap, I suggest that you see the "big picture" and thereby the path that will lead you to your set goals. Stories of entrepreneurial success teach us that a leap of thought or a change in the entrepreneur's thinking is important for progress. Don't forget - companies aren't buildings, machines and other equipment. Companies are people who share your responsibility for success. A capable and committed team that is part of the company's success story is of the utmost importance.

- **People and their relationships**

The bigger the company becomes in terms of the number of employees, the more difficult it is to maintain a genuine relationship between the employees. This is especially true for the relationship between management personnel and positions in production. The problem can be solved with an efficient management organisation, divided into three levels: management or top management, heads of departments or middle management and team leaders within the departments. Developing open communication is what makes heads

of departments different from managing directors. The former know how to listen to their colleagues on all levels - this is key to a successful company and satisfied workers. Whereas it is the top management's duty to train several heads of departments to develop a suitable mentoring programme within the company.
Smaller companies usually think that they're too small for this process and that they don't require it. But, such organisation exists whether the company wants it or not. Organisational methods have been around since the beginning of civilisation, whether it was tasks related to hunting, gathering or something else. Management and organisation are the requirements for the beginning and the conclusion of the process; in small and big companies. This means both as regards the technical side of production and the natural life-cycles.
- **Physical growth and pushing for independence**

There are two key areas regarding a company's growth. The first area is a physical increase in spatial capacities (production halls and offices) and the second is becoming independent from the business functions mentioned earlier. Assigning business functions from one person to several people is a very demanding moment in a company's development due to the increased workload. We are faced with the requirements of concrete leadership and skills, and the tasks of supervision and monitoring. Often, the quickest solution is educating managers through workshops within the company or private coaching. The visible consequences are numerous complications and, often, reduced business performance What is needed is detailed preparation and careful deliberation, which could save the company a lot of energy and financial means. The pitfalls of the key areas can be controlled well using the tools mentioned. Of course, that doesn't mean you will never run aground on the way. Let me comfort you. It will happen - several times - but you'll be able to find the right path by using the tools described.

- **Brain drain**

When a company's growth is in the ascendance, its owners and managing directors start to worry about how to keep their excellent employees from leaving for other companies. A good and common example of a solution to this is a co-ownership scheme. The reason for such a solution is the fact that a salary as a physical doctrine doesn't "feed" the human ego enough, which is yearning for recognition. A share in the company, and thereby recognition of equality in co-creating the company, gives employees exactly that. In this case, management is quite complex so it will be dealt with in the dedicated chapter dedicated.

3.3 BRAINSTORMING

I mentioned this tool when describing how to develop a business idea; here I provide a more detailed description and present its use in practice.

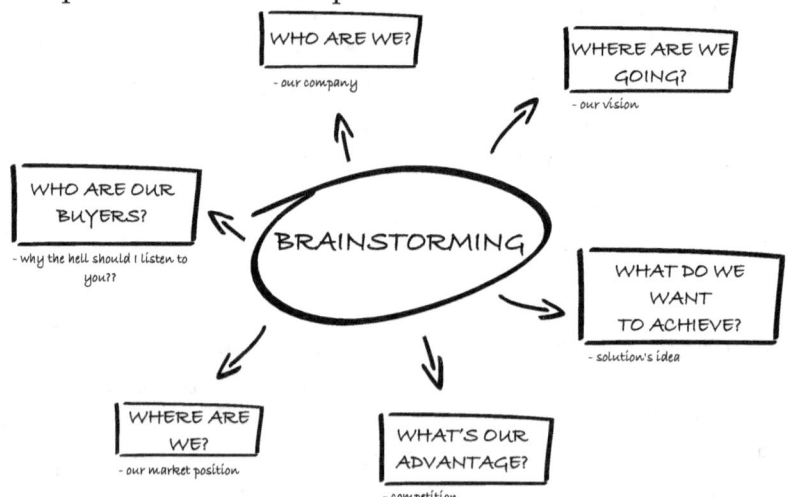

Mind map 7: Brainstorming

Answers to these questions will become your concrete solution. All key players in the company or department should go through and answer the questions independently. Afterwards, hold a meeting at which you will combine all the opinions and establish the actual state. I suggest that you hold this meeting as a brainstorming session (which it is) and you hire an external coordinator who will ensure appropriate communication and prevent any conflicts arising from participants' differing views.

3.4 ANALYSIS TOOLS

Our past experiences are one of the key ways to prevent us from making the same mistakes again. But experiences on their own, without analysing or establishing the reason for the complication or the unsuccessful realisation, don't bring about the change we want. It is often hard to make a subjective analysis, and it therefore makes sense to consult an expert in this field who has no connection to the case at hand. The help or analysis itself can be carried out by asking the right questions, which should be as concrete and practical as possible.

- Write down your company's main goals and, as far as you can remember, the date when you last renewed them.
- What challenges are you facing in concrete areas (technology, finances, business operations optimisation) that are part of the company's main goals?
- Which activities have you recently performed to overcome these challenges?
- What were the results of the activities performed?
- Do you think you are doing better; if so, why?
- Are you currently facing any great tests within the company (current state, on today's date)?
- In your opinion, what do you need to resolve the issue?
- What are the substitutes or the competition on the market like?

- Are you too cheap or too expensive?
- Do your sales channels (resellers, agents or shops) fail to earn enough in real time, which leaves them unmotivated?
- Are you offering your solution to the wrong people?
- Have you elaborated an upsale?
- How many events have you organised and what's the difference in price?
- Are sales more demanding and are you understaffed for efficient sales?
- Are you underprepared for sales and do you spend too long with your customers with regard to sales effects?
- Do you choose the wrong words at the wrong time?

You can use this tested tool on your own, but I suggest finding help from an external person who isn't part of the company and isn't "infected" with the business you're dealing in. What you need is to recognise and obtain concrete solutions as quickly as possible so that they can help you with concrete challenges. The fields of technology and finances differ in this area from the field of utilising existing sales resources. The field you are learning about in this book is the method of attracting new customers, teaching you how to carry out and measure successful sales activities and, thereby, controlling the tasks performed.

3.5 IT'S ALSO GOOD TO TALK TO YOURSELF

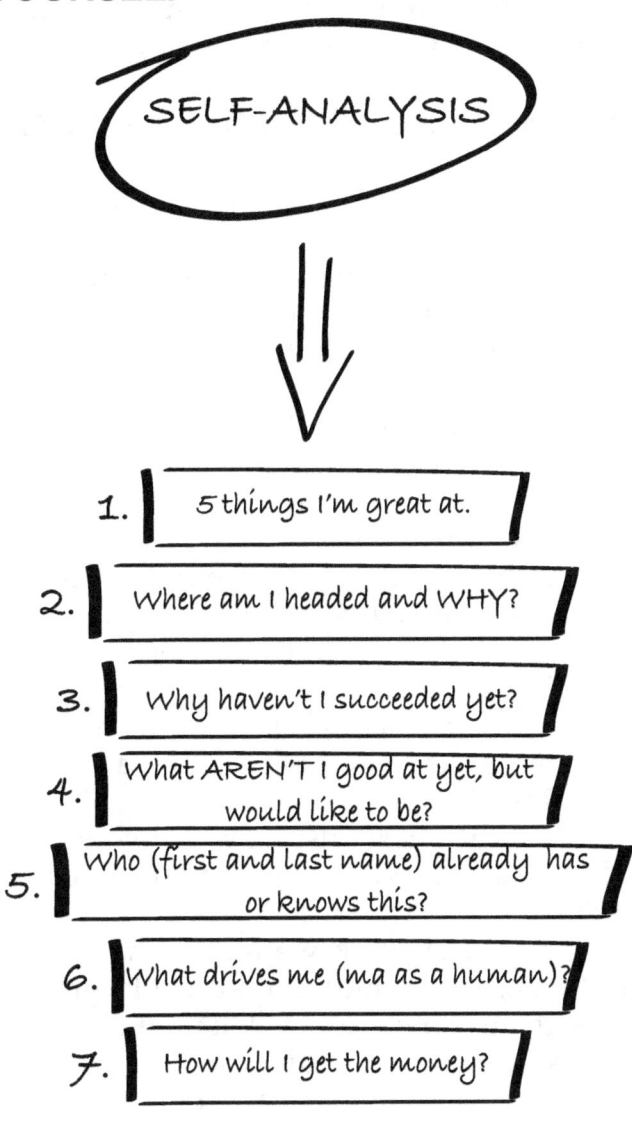

Mind map 8: Self-analysis

As I emphasised before, it is necessary that a company's owners and managing directors clarify what their own and the company's goals are. The same goes for salespeople. You can do this by conducting a self-analysis that is also a required part of the self-motivation process. The following sample briefly presents how, by conducting self-analysis, you can ensure that you are not an obstacle to your company's development.

The naked truth: An example of using sales tools

An example of the sales stages of a transport company:

- 1st period: Start off with a narrow focus. Buy a van and find 16 potential clients (your goal is to get at least 4 regular customers). Use the tools:

  - Who are your buyers? Those with smaller shipments? Those who don't trust courier services because they rely on 100% delivery at a specified time.
  - Who is truly a customer? Emphasise the added values: 100% delivery at the right time, fastest delivery without complications or breaks, possibility of immediately returning other segments or packaging material; if their main condition is the lowest price, they are not your customers.
  - Ask the right questions: How are you dealing with this today? What happens if the goods are late?
  - Solution: In our work we follow the "just in time" rule, which means that newly produced products are delivered to your buyers as soon as possible. It's important for us to have available vans (even though you have just one at the start) and rested staff who are ready for urgent deliveries. We are well aware that our customers wish to use their strengths, i.e. quality and quick delivery, as a competitive advantage over other providers.
  - Conclusion: Emphasise a reference. Propose a

trial period to your potential partners and ask if you can provide a few urgent deliveries for them.
- Additional sales: Don't start yet. Once the trial period is over, offer the customer smaller urgent transports for delivery of goods or any other urgent deliveries in their vicinity - offer everything as a package, as this way you'll get a buyer who buys your service "daily" - this is good for strengthening your relationship with the business partner and for a favourable cash flow.
- 2nd period: Focus and good customer responses will open up possibilities for development. If your solution is a proven success and your customers accept it as the best solution, you don't need to be afraid of investing in development. The only trap that might lay ahead is your capable colleagues. Only those with the same values, meaning that you can teach them every step crucial to gaining a competitive advantage, are suitable for management roles in your company. If you grow too quickly and can't find the right colleagues, you could even ruin your company or your otherwise excellent solution.
- 3rd period: Competition in transportation and courier services is very strong, which means that the market is well developed. It could happen to anyone that while developing the business, certain mistakes are made in a particular market. A common mistake is to select the wrong people or use the cheapest, but often irresponsible, workforce (young students or retired people). There's always a chance you might make a mistake in a micro area. The expansion of development in logistics continues from direct deliveries to

groupage transport (e.g. regular connections with bigger cities where smaller shipments are transported using one vehicle) and to remote groupage depots or logistics centres. While companies which deal in production or sales integrate their own logistics services, external entrepreneurs have the chance to prove the competitive advantage of "outsourcing" these services.

- 4th period: Strengthening your trademark means that the main players in your area are using your services. Focusing on the selected area and continuous development is the only way to strengthen your position and advance your business. Most importantly, you have to think about what else your existing customers might need. It could be simple things like documented efficiency, faster marking, and delivery several times a day. What's important are the details that bring down costs or increase competitive advantage for your customer.
- 5th period: The saying goes: "A big tree attracts the woodsman's axe." Once you've reached all corners of the market, many competitive companies (especially big ones) will show interest in you. First, they will try copying your solution. The bigger ones will attempt price dumping. Your next task is either to buy the competition or be sold to the competition. If your vision is long lasting and clear, and you have people who would love to continue your business, you should expand your business. Don't expect expansion to new, unknown customers on a competitive market. Every time you expand, this means you will take someone else's piece of the pie. The competitive fight will thus intensify and you will have to find

your place on the market, otherwise you'll be out. If you're bored and don't see yourself in this business in the long run, don't wait. Find potential buyers for the company as soon as you can. When doing so, first check who has the money and is successful. The best time to complete the sale is once you've made your decision, and not once this is one of the possible solutions.

3.6 PRACTICAL PART: SALES TOOLS

Task 1: Prepare a five-point business plan.

Task 2: Write down your personal vision, goals and customers who are in line with this vision.

Task 3: Think about and write down how you could improve your vision and thereby optimise your goals.

Task 4: Check your price differential.

Task 5: Prepare an external test of your business vision.

Task 6: Prepare an activity plan.

Task 7: Evaluate your work from the adopted decision onwards.

3.7 IN BRIEF: SALES TOOLS

1. As a salesperson, you need to know how to develop a business idea.
2. Use sales tools in your business processes.
3. Stick to sales steps in your business processes.
4. Remember, a good idea that no one wants to buy is just a good idea.
5. Be aware of entrepreneurial stages and their pitfalls.
6. Analysis tools are the main and most important sales tools.

4. THERE ARE NO SALES WITHOUT CLIENTS

Selling is a meeting between a salesperson and a buyer, an event which should leave both of them feeling satisfied. Everything starts with us, i.e. what our attitude to our business is, how successful our business is, and this is how people around us perceive us. Bear in mind that the client is the first in line who makes the sale possible. This means that you need to pay all your attention to the client and their wishes.

4.1 WHO ARE YOUR BUYERS

However... People around us aren't just buyers. They can be observers who at that moment aren't yet buyers. With a professional attitude, you can make a good impression on an observing passer-by. Once they decide to buy, they'll probably think of you. Efficient thinking about your business starts based on problems (pains) that your solutions solve for your buyers. Thinking about your product or solution will lead you to determining the sales philosophy behind selling your solution.
You can do so by carefully thinking about your solution in connection with your buyers. As you learned in the previous chapter, this is done by using various sales tools.

This careful consideration has two effects:

1. the development department is able to understand the challenges your buyers have, and

2. the sales department is able to define the questions and answers to be used in sales presentations to explain what is needed to the buyer so that they decide to buy your solution.

Mind map 9: Who are our buyers?

Thinking about your buyer is more efficient if you imagine them as a concrete person. This means thinking about your potential buyers' age, lifestyle, their professional relationship, what line of business they're in, where do they hang out, what area do they have in common etc. You need to visualise potential buyers. For example: you can imagine your ideal buyer, a man, 35 years old, an engineer in a project company, very precise and aesthetic, likes nice things, his favourite colour is blue, goes cycling and sailing in his time off, is married and has school-age children. This way, it will be easier to think what this person might like, where they feel the most comfortable, what their values and beliefs are. If you're unable to answer some of these questions, turn to a person who could give you the answers. To a person who you think is like your buyer. A detailed buyer analysis is necessary in order to reach the first meaningful conclusion in helping you establish why your buyers decide to buy your solution/product and in what moment they do so.

4.2 SALES VIA AGENTS AND DISTRIBUTORS

It is hard to convince a client to buy using only words, images, actions and samples. Think about it, there's never enough advertising material and there are lots of rubbish products on the market with good advertising material - this has made buyers immune to it or take it with a pinch of salt. Whenever you talk about tools for helping you work with partners, stick to the presumption that your solutions or products are excellent. This means you understand that they're an efficient solution to some open questions or "pains" that buyers on the market have. Before you build a solid business relationship, you have to sell your solution and service to your partner. For this, the sales pitch won't be the same as when talking to your buyer; a lot more needs to be covered. You need to address open questions that are much more specific and are a consequence of your agent or distributor's communication with the buyer. An agent or distributor will rarely forward buyers' questions that you haven't already encountered. These questions are usually the same and very frequent. That is why you need to educate your business representatives and prepare them for the relevant questions. You should do this with the help of sales tools; hire an expert to do even better than that. Your representatives will benefit greatly from such preparation since they will be able to answer any questions (that you pointed out) the buyer might have at a sales meeting; this way, they will win over the buyer and gain confidence themselves, which will, in turn, bring you profit. This can be called a win-win-win situation, where everyone wins. You as the provider, the agent as the representative and the buyer as the customer. Remember, you're not only selling your solution to your sales representatives, you're also offering them a partnership.

4.3 WHO IS AN AGENT AND WHO IS A DISTRIBUTOR

There is an obvious difference between an agent and a distributor. That's why it's important that the person responsible for the former or the latter sales representative is well acquainted with the agreements and provisions of a partnership contract. Usually, everyone involved has the same interest - i.e. to sell the solution on the market and earn money doing so. But, this is not everything. In addition to the business part of the relationship, there is also an interpersonal, human part of it. I've kept an amicable relationship with all my business partners all over the world. This means that I often call them and, if possible, pay them a visit. Business is created by people and this will probably never change.

An agent represents the company in a particular market, and negotiates with the buyer up to a point authorised by the company. The agent often endorses the same sales process as the parent company they represent. They win contracts and orders due to the name and on behalf of the company represented. They are paid by the company they represent after the business is concluded and paid for. In short this is called a commission. An agent is an extended arm of the sales department in a distant market. They represent the company in their domestic market and perform sales activities in return for a commission from the value of the sales. An agent is an ambassador of the company and has to, therefore, look the part and share the company's values.

Unlike an agent, a distributor is a representative of the company in their market who buys solutions from the company for a reduced price and then sells them on their account. A distributor is thus a legal person who collaborates with you by buying your solutions from you. They can keep stock in a warehouse or showroom. All contracts with the end buyers are made on their own behalf and they don't hide the fact that your company is their supplier. A business contract is concluded with a distributor, in which the collaboration is defined in detail. In some cases an exclusive contract is signed with the distributor, which means that no one else, not even the salesperson themselves, is allowed to sell solutions or products on the market stipulated in the business cooperation contract without the distributor's knowledge. If a deal is made without including the distributor, they are entitled to a specific exclusive commission.

Selecting an agent or a distributor is challenging since you have to consider your partner's professional knowledge, their recognisability on the market that they control, their sales abilities, the representative's work habits, integrity and personal desire to succeed. You have to take note of the facts you've noticed, check references and, most importantly, listen to your intuition.

Every buyer expects to receive the solution that you sold them. You knew at the start of the sale that you could prepare your solution and that it would solve your buyer's challenge. It is important that you've convinced the buyer to buy your solution with the help of arguments, successfully completed tests and references.

You main task when collaborating with agents and distributors is to sell them a relationship. This means that you act like a partner, you respond quickly and professionally and that you're always available to them. You need to offer them support that will give them the feeling of not being alone and of having your backing. The biggest mistake many companies make is keeping a distributor waiting and not replying to them straight away since they are just a distributor, earning money on "their" account. If that's your attitude, don't forget that you're not alone on the market and that the distributor can always change supplier. Distributors have to "buy" your solutions, your company. This means that you have to sell them the belief that it's pleasant to do business with you and highly profitable. Your relationship with agents and distributors can't be any different than the one you have with your direct buyers. After all, your representatives are also your buyers.

The naked truth: An example of business communication with a representative of a company

"Dear Mr. Smith. We discussed every detail of our references and technology. Since you're the expert, I don't wish to lecture you on the added value of our solutions.
But you're probably interested in the financial side of collaborating with us.
Your commission for the acquired and completed business amounts to 20% of the contract value.
For forwarding a more complex enquiry where a direct meeting with the client is required, your contact

commission is 2% since the sales amounts are usually much higher."

4.4 BUYERS' AREAS

On the basis of your previous experiences and in line with your commercial philosophy you've got to know the areas your buyers come from. The most efficient way of organising your work with agents or distributors is to define these areas in as much detail as possible. The simplest way to define the areas is by using buyer analysis tools; the areas can thus be divided into three main groups:

- Sponsor: user of a solution in a B2B process; for example: Head of production needs a solution - a machine - and has to explain this need to the managing director, who is the decision-maker.
- Decision-maker: managing director or the person who will make the decision if the investment isn't planned in advance.
- Purchasing officer: person who is often looking for added value in sales conditions (discounts, payment due date, instalments).

Being able to recognise and define your buyers' areas using an analysis will save you valuable time you would've otherwise spent in meetings with non-key people in the companies to which you sell your solutions.

4.5 BUYER'S COMMERCIAL PHILOSOPHY

For a deeper understanding of the buyer, you need to know your buyer's commercial philosophy. Put yourself in their shoes and ask yourself:

1. Who are our buyers?
2. What problems are being solved by our solution or product?
3. Why are they buying our solution?
4. What are the permanent consequences / feelings of our buyers?
5. What else has been newly developed to "make their lives easier"?

Preparing a commercial philosophy for an individual solution is therefore crucial. Every answer to each question will change your view as it might show you whether your potential customer understands you correctly or not. This kind of thinking and patience will help you as it will prevent things happening by chance in the future - instead, you will be awaiting them and in control of them.

The naked truth: Example of our solutions' field of use

- Oil pipes - oil company with a strong and globally dispersed distribution network is looking for a solution for efficient pipe assembly in oil well drilling.
- Alternative artists and restorers - wood press - small art studio with a focus on baroque sideboard restoration, usually an important player at the London Art Fair and a global distributor of solutions for wealthy antique collectors.

4.6 HOW TO INTENSIVELY LOOK FOR CLIENTS

It's easiest to catch fish where there's plenty of them, right? Similar is true for finding new clients - as mentioned in the section on commercial philosophy. So, you need to find out who your potential clients are and where they are. Agents or distributors can also find this kind of information using your established system; each in their market.

The methods of acquiring new clients can vary depending on the market; the same way as people's cultures and habits do.

But one fact is true in every part of the world - if you're looking for buyers, you'll find them. You can advise your agents or distributors on a tested method for intensively finding new buyers only after you've tried many things. As mentioned, you also need to sell your business to your distributors. This means sharing your methods for getting new buyers in a specific market. After all, distributors and agents are selling for you. Showing them how to carry out the business they are selling for you is part of the lesson. This means it is useful if you help your representative as they take their first steps towards getting buyers and carrying out sales. This way you will motivate your agents and distributors, which will help them become highly successful representatives of your company.

4.7 FIRST CONTACT WITH A CLIENT

You won't close the deal in the first five minutes after meeting your client, but you could lose it. Your non-verbal communication reveals a lot. Your posture, tone of voice and the text you need to say with enthusiasm to convey your genuine desire to help people.

This is also part of the know-how, which is very important for your further success. You don't have to worry that you'll be revealing a big business secret. Your most important mission is to sell or increase sales. That's why you should adapt your presentation and questions for your customer to the vocabulary of your product's language. This means your sentences should be prepared in detail, but also be logical so that they awaken logical consecutive questions in the person you're talking to, the answers to which they will find in your solution.

The naked truth: An example of first contact with a buyer

Often, salespeople don't know how to make the first contact with their buyers, especially if they are unknown people in strictly business relationships. You shouldn't be afraid of saying directly what you are doing here or of presenting your solution directly. This technique is often very useful at fairs and conferences where you have to communicate the essence to many potential buyers.

For example: "Hello! My name's Robert. I come from XYZ Tech. Technologists often wonder how to remove residue resulting from transformer treatment in the fastest and most economically efficient way. For this purpose, we have carefully designed and tested at several different institutes at home and abroad our new solution called 'erosion with xyz dust'. Using a technologically advanced process the potential residues are already removed during treatment, which means that the solution also acts as a cooling additive. It solves the problem of potential residues or spots on transformers. In addition, the dust is non-conductive and ecologically sound. A certain percentage of the 'xyz dust' can be recycled. This means it can be used several times, up to 4-times in a cycle. This is why you also need (cross selling) the 'ZYX filter' recycling device, which, according to known data in practice, provides a return on investment within 150 working hours."

Your presentation should be "naked", in other words, it should have "balls". This means you should invest all of your current energy in it and fascinate your potential buyer. Why? Because others will do the same. A well-prepared and professional presentation should be clear, concise and directed towards the expected goals so that in it your client can recognise their "pain". When it comes to longer presentations, explain to your business partner that your business process includes time for presentation (where you talk a lot) and time for asking questions (where you talk as little as possible). Finish your presentation by gathering as much concrete information from your client as possible as this will enable you to prepare a quote that will be acceptable for the client.

4.8 SELLING COMPLEX SOLUTIONS AND CLIENTS

In essence, selling complex solutions doesn't differ much from selling simple solutions and products; what's different is that selling complex solutions demands more iterations of the sales steps and thereby greater complexity in using sales tools.
Selling complex solutions usually isn't done after one meeting or sales pitch; it takes a string of carefully planned meetings that demand different preparation from the salesperson.

First meeting

One of the main elements in getting new business is the so-called "first meeting".
When you arrive at a first meeting, you need to observe all the "rules" of business communication and appearance we discussed in the previous chapters of this book. It's also important that you ask your client the following questions:

1. How are you resolving this issue today?
2. So you wish to improve this, have you perhaps

thought about how...?
3. If I understand you correctly, the problem you wish to resolve is quite serious?
4. Perhaps someone else in your company is affected by these challenges, someone who could join us in our discussion?
5. Make a summary of what you've discussed and set a date for your next meeting, where you'll present your solution.

Remind your salespeople that the way you ask questions is very important and crucial for establishing whether you're talking to a "real" potential client or someone you can't help. The client shouldn't feel like they're answering questions from a survey, instead they should feel like they are simply talking to a person. It's very important to stay quiet during conversation and not put words in their mouth since you won't get the picture you need to prepare your quote. The primary goal is to encourage thinking about the problem the potential buyer is experiencing. This way they can, while answering your questions, realise that they need a partner to solve their challenge.

Preparation for a second meeting

At the end of your previous meeting, you and your client set the exact date for your next meeting. You also asked (with a sort of "disguise") who, besides the person you're talking to, will co-decide whether they buy your solution or not.
That's why it's extremely important how you go about your next meeting. Ask your new discussion partner the same questions listed above, since it might happen that they don't think the same way or are not experiencing the problem in the same way as their colleague. Usually, the issue described won't be completely the opposite, yet it is important to get answers to these key questions

from the person you've just met as well. In the second part of the meeting, present your solution in the form of a quote. What's very important here is organisation itself; that's why it's better if you don't prepare the quote yourself, but have someone else prepare it for you. If organisation is poor, quotes often arrive to the customer late (too late), and salespeople are unable to follow up due to work overload.

The programme for carrying out the next meeting is thus carefully planned so that your business partner, who you're training for successful business operations, knows every detail of their next step; in practice, this means that everyone who is participating in the project is informed about the next meeting and the subsequent activities.

4.9 PRACTICAL PART: CLIENTS

Task 1: *For a given product and solution, write down who your buyers are.*

Task 2: *For your company, write down who your buyers are.*

Task 3: *For a given solution, think about how you would sell it via agents and distributors.*

Task 4: *For a given solution, write down your buyers' areas.*

Task 5: *For a given solution, write down how to intensively look for buyers.*

Task 6: *For a given solution, write down five points for preparing for your first meeting.*

Task 7: *For a given solution, write down five points for preparing for your second meeting.*

4.10 IN BRIEF: CLIENTS

1. Find out who your buyers are.
2. Expand your sales via agents and distributors.
3. Define potential clients' areas: sponsor, decision-maker, purchasing officer.
4. What problems does your solution solve?
5. Learn how to intensively look for new clients.
6. Learn how to make first contact with a client.
7. Complex solutions contain all the sales steps and are carried out in several sales cycles.
8. Prepare well for your first meeting.

5. SALES CLOSING

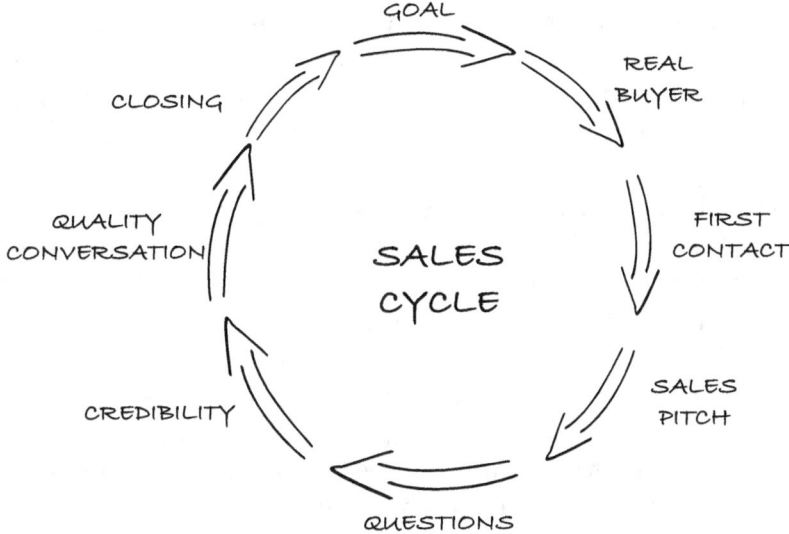

Mind map 10: The sales cycle

5.1 PRACTICE = SUCCESSFUL SALES

Often, successful salespeople know how to find new buyers and prepare an excellent presentation, but what they're lacking is a sales result. Problems with closing sales can occur due to complex sales prices or the salesperson simply being too embarrassed to ask the customer what they think of their quote. There are also others causes for poor sales closing, but remember, by using the right sales steps and correct sales tools, the salesperson can control these causes and use them to their benefit.
This way you can always ask the buyer what they think of your quote. Hard work and the effort you invest, free-of-charge, with the desire to sell something gives you the right to hear your customer's opinion on the proposed quote. In part, this depends on where you're

selling, but in some parts of the world it is simply impossible not to get an answer to that question. If you think that the client only wants to receive a quote from you in order to put pressure on their already selected provider, you can check that by asking for additional information. Ask your client for photographs or design plans or invite them to visit your company to examine the process. The important thing is that they do something. They will respect you only as much as you respect yourself.

Don't allow yourself to spend several hours preparing a quote that won't even get the chance to compete in the final round. If the client makes the effort and provides you with additional information, you were wrong as well. This way you'll be able to prepare a solution no one will be able to beat. The client has thus "earned" your quote, and it is now up to you to prove to them that you're different and show them the advantages on the basis of the quote you've prepared.

Observing the client

While you elegantly deal with business communication and client observation, you can use the following sentence: "I've noticed that I haven't explained something well enough. What are you worried about? Can I explain this some more?"

If your client is taking a long time to think about your quote, this sentence is important to encourage decision making. Some might think that the buyer would reject you if you say this. Rejection is definitely better than creating false hope and additional calls, visits and testing costs. It is always possible that the solution isn't suitable and is not what they had expected. It is also always possible that they are interested in the quote, but it's out of their reach and they're having a difficult time saying "No". You need to be able to recognise this and adapt your quote so that it fits both situations.

Sales Closing

Observing the client gives you a very useful advantage and it's worth developing this technique for the needs of successful sales as well as the needs of everyday life. By observing ourselves, our surroundings, objects, vehicles, production areas and a company's general image, you can establish what kind of values the people running the company have. I remember some companies where all work processes had to be stopped and the place tidied up for a few days before a business delegation visited. I think a company's tidiness can be compared to personal hygiene and, in a time and place where the usual standard is good enough for a comfortable life, comparable to integrity, frankness and respect to business partners.

By using the client observation technique, I often analyse the person and the company I'm visiting and make an advanced assessment of how our collaboration will turn out. My first impressions are rarely wrong.
An entrepreneur who doesn't want to show you their production area, something we are usually proud of, is hiding something. You might think this has to do with the client's big know-how secrets - but that's not the case, as no one expects the host to show them every corner of their company.

Once, I participated in a business meeting for motor oil manufacturers in Texas as the client's representative. During the whole week's visit with the potential business partner I only saw meeting rooms and offices - no production area. They showed me photos of their production area, but it wasn't hard to see that the machines and the people's clothes in the photos were over thirty years old. I warned them several times that we wouldn't be able to continue our collaboration unless I saw at least a warehouse or distribution centre. Unfortunately they didn't do that and despite very efficient presentations and successful tests, we couldn't continue our collaboration. Since this was a meeting of several potential business partners, the manufacturer lost the business with us as well as with representatives of other markets. Even when you are at the start of your business journey and you really don't have much to show, explain this to your buyers; your presentation, professional knowledge and passion will convince your client to at least give you a chance and prove yourself. Usually, the only way people know how to show off their success is by using our external "shields". I could say in a "naked" way - we're seeing who's got a bigger one. "External shields" are things such as cars, clothing, jewellery, shoes, bags, computers, phones etc. The things we want people to notice, that we usually touch often while talking. This can come across as unprofessional and unprepared. Our appearance is important, especially when our solution is of high-quality and perhaps in the higher price range. Which means - always, as this is how you should perceive your solution. If you don't, you will not be or aren't a successful salesperson.

I'd like to point out a mistake common to many salespeople - they notice and comment too soon. For example, if they notice that the person they're speaking to has photographs of sail boats on their office walls and is also wearing deck shoes to work, which clearly indicates their great passion and hobby, they ask them at the first meeting: "Do you have a sail boat?" By doing so they've dug themselves into a hole, since the person they're talking to will go on about this in detail, leaving them very little time for their sales pitch.

In spite of this, this kind of question should be asked at meetings to strengthen the trust and business friendship or to connect with the client. I'd like to mention an interesting fact - in some markets (for example in Russia) it might happen that your client gives you a lift with "their" car, when in fact it isn't theirs at all (as you will discover). It will be either too clean, without a sun glasses case, paper tissues, receipts or any of the paraphernalia that you might notice even in a very tidy person's car. And so you can conclude that your client wants to make a really good impression on you since they want you to see them as a very successful entrepreneur. On the other hand you may notice someone who wears their shirt untucked and calls themselves "creative", when really they're just scruffy.

Adapting to the client

In meetings, an unforeseen situation may often occur or the conversation does not go as planned. In order to turn the sales meeting to your advantage despite this, you need to know how to adapt to your client. You can do this with a few simple steps:

- Monitor non-verbal signs.
- Try to recognise their values and adapt.
- Mention your client's lifestyle and hobbies.
- Be specific.
- Don't take refusals personally; instead, try to adapt your quote or solution to your client's wishes.

Pain

While opening the pain when talking to the client and presenting them the potential solutions, you should implement a pre-prepared sales closing plan. The reasons for sales process failure lie also in skipping certain sales closing steps. When you make a decision instead of the client, even if you do so unintentionally, this can upset the client and they might react negatively to your quote. Unfortunately, by doing so, you're doing your competitor a big favour.
We usually start using non-verbal communication when we don't believe in something. The buyer recognises

this as a warning that something isn't ok.

The reasons are often complex. Due to the wrong sales approach or not enough training, the salesperson is unable to recognise the benefits of the solution they are selling. This leads to doubts appearing in their subconsciousness, which convince them that their product is too expensive for the situation being solved. This often happens to less experienced salespeople after they've been rejected by potential buyers several times in a row. The term sales price complex applies when the salesperson thinks that the price of the solution or the product they are selling is too high or that the solution or the product isn't worth the money. The salesperson usually sees the world through their own prism or the events around them. Your potential buyers do not necessarily share your thinking. In the end, we're just people. To survive we eat, wash, work etc., and we do this in various ways and in various conditions depending on our status in society. That's why it's important to know your commercial philosophy, which precisely defines your buyers and their habits. Getting rid of the price complex is an important decision and realisation. If a salesperson is unable to accept this, despite help from other people, they should change their field of work or the solution they're selling.

Preparing for objections

If your client's objection (which you haven't thought of yet) catches you by surprise, the meeting was certainly a success as you learned something new. You might not have been aware of the comments since you hadn't thought about this enough or missed a gap in the real world. Such cases rarely happen to professional entrepreneurs. If you experience realistic objections, this means that you haven't prepared your presentation very well; the client should have learned all about the benefits of your solution in your presentation. The most common objections arise when the buyer has already decided not to buy the solution or they are connected to the competition's quote. In such cases, preparing for objections is crucial. As in every business, to ensure a successful closing you need to strengthen your solution and your professional expertise by answering your client's questions. Good preparation includes objections from your competitors that aren't essential to successfully resolving the client's problem. To answer such objections, use provable facts affecting technological or economic questions. Remember, you should never mention your competitor by name. To avoid this, use the term "another provider".

Another crucial preparation for objections includes expertise. If you're dealing with the pharmaceutical, cosmetic, chemical or other industry that has a strong impact on the environment, you need to learn all the terms of the ingredients, the chemical reactions when substances come into contact with other substances etc. I disagree with those who think a salesperson needs to be an expert in chemical or other engineering fields. Anyone can learn enough about this micro area to not talk nonsense or make a fool of themselves in the sales process. If you're talking to a distinguished expert in the micro field in question, who is asking you detailed technological questions to increase their reputation in the eyes of those present at the meeting, tell them that you'll get them their answer from one of your development experts.

The biggest advantage of a sales meeting is the possibility to announce obtaining certain technical additions - a technical expert is unable to do so as an immediate answer is expected of them. At a business meeting for presenting the solution it often happens that a customer, who is also the sole decision-maker,

stops the negotiations and wishes to buy the solution. In a more complex sales process, the decision-making process usually takes a bit longer. As I already mentioned, the salesperson should take a step back and let the client
breathe before they make their decision. You should also teach your partners, agents or distributors to act in line with your company's code of conduct and with respect to your clients or buyers.

A suitable tool for a meeting where a sales closing (favourable to your company) must happen, is called "overcoming objections".

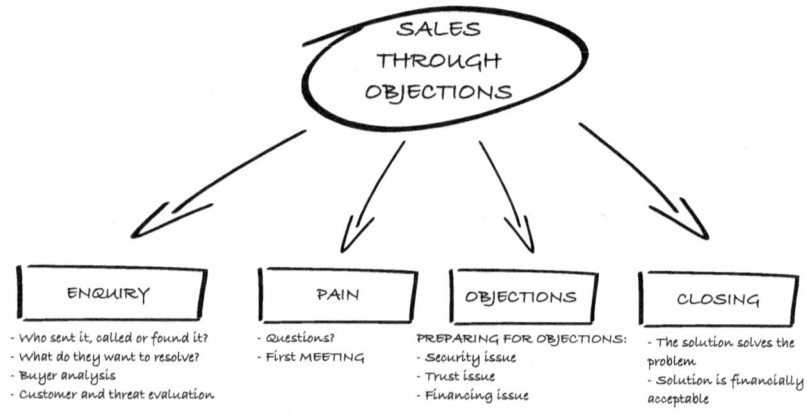

Mind map 11: Sales through objections

Sales is not a scam

As a salesperson you'll often find yourself in a situation where someone tells you that you only want to cheat or "screw" them with your solution. It can also happen that you will ask yourself this question, since trying to convince people in sales meetings can be very tiring and often just a game of words which leads to nowhere. You should know this is also part of sales. Even though sales isn't usually referred to as the "world's oldest profession", you could call it that. If you understand that, your clients will understand it also. What is important is that you stick to your personal and business principles.

5.2 CLOSING THE SALE IS THE MOST IMPORTANT PART

We could say that sales are done by people and "closings". Even though we do everything right and the buyer likes our solution, something usually goes wrong at the end. Without closing the sale, there is no sale. This doesn't mean you haven't earned any money; it means a loss for you since you spent a lot of your time and other resources trying to win over this client. Closing the sales cycle is its most important part. Actually, this is the only part where you have to do everything right; in other words, you can do everything else wrong, as long as you close the deal correctly.

There are only two possible results in closing - Yes or No. All other endings are excuses. Those of you who disagree with this sentence know it also. It is like buying a Ferrari without any money. You can dream about it, but you can't buy it.

Closing the sale is when the salesperson should be completely quiet. If you wish to help by talking and putting words in their mouth, they might see this as imposing or as another way of "screwing them over". You had enough time to talk and to convince them; now it's time to leave the decision to the buyer.

Closing sales is what brings money to the company and enables it to grow. Sales closing is what distinguishes a successful salesperson from a non-successful one. Advertising materials and presentations aren't essential. They are important insofar as they get you to the right closing. Closing sales tells you if the solution is right, if it's presented correctly and if it's something users are looking for. This means, you can learn on the basis of sales closings. If you can get feedback from the

customer, even though they rejected your quote, you can amend your solution and improve it.
Sales closings usually bring us to three realisations:

- Number one - are we even talking to a suitable client?
- Number two - are they even interested in the solution to the problem/challenges?
- Number three – a concluded agreement or question posed in various forms: would you buy it?

All three realisations are very important for subsequent sales since they give us the opportunity to improve. I would also like to point out that a salesperson should pass on any feedback received to their company's management. Many salespeople don't do this. A true salesperson works well with the management and development teams. Getting feedback at meetings should be a salesperson's main activity and motive in addition to the sales closing.

5.3 SALES STEPS TO REACH CLOSING

In your sales steps beware of generous discounting. If you receive a high discount very easily, you ask yourself if there's something wrong with the quality. Some salespeople decide to offer the maximum discount at the start, which is like giving up. You should move to a deal's economic side, i.e. discounts, once you're certain that you've won over the buyer.

If you're selling a simple consumer product, and you've skipped the technical part, the best discount you can offer is offering another item. You should say something like:

"If you buy ten items, you get one free of charge."

When it comes to broader consumer products, sales quantity means success. Manufacturing such products is cheapest if it's done twenty-four hours a day, every day of the year. The effect of a financial discount isn't as beneficial as selling "three for the price of two".

Discounts have to be earned, and the size of the discount is decided subjectively by the salesperson. Usually, the salesperson will decide on their own to what level they will let the price fall. Some companies employ negotiators in their purchasing departments. Such experts are paid on the basis of their ability to lower providers' prices. Of course, this is also part of sales and is no different to other parts. Lowering prices is very subjective, meaning that it very much depends on the salesperson's current well-being. When your monthly realisation is poor or when you're making the deal of a lifetime, you'll be very indulgent. I understand you completely as I have been in your situation many times. But you should think about your integrity. The negotiator or buyer may insult you as a person - this is your personal choice; but you can never allow them to insult the quality of the product and the company you're representing. When the boundaries of good taste are crossed, you mustn't give up and become the victim. If you're a fraudulent salesperson, you will get caught one day and you will lose your good name. The same is true, if you give in and accept inappropriate communication. It will be very difficult for you to change your position in the business society later on.

As mentioned before, every salesperson should talk to themselves often and answer the following questions: "Who are you? Who do you want to become? How would you like other people to perceive you?" Such moments are very useful for such questions since we will answer them most honestly in difficult sales situations. I recommend writing down your answers and occasionally checking them. This a very useful tool for life.

Preparing for objections is key. A well-prepared salesperson has already answered all the potential objections during the presentation. Objections are not to be seen as an attack on you, the salesperson. The "complaint" is usually based on a misunderstanding, disagreement over the price or is simply a case of the wrong solution for the client in question. If you think the objection is rhetorical or doubtful, simply ask:

"Why do you think so?" Some customers are always pessimistic. They make comments and sometimes end up arguing with themselves. I've experienced a number of similar cases - a good solution, which I was too afraid to use when I was younger, is to say: "So, what do you propose we do now?" Eighty percent of those who "moan" will decide to buy upon hearing this question. As you get more experienced, you will learn that people's nature differs from one customer to the next.

Selling is like dancing. The salesperson leads so that the customer enjoys their "dance" and is, in the end, delighted with their purchase. Allow your customer to become confident by presenting the rules
of the "dance" in advance and setting the steps.
Selling is not deceiving or scamming; and if the buyer feels this way you'll be able to repeat it many times.
Let's recap. A good salesperson only has one face and one name; you should therefore guard it carefully and protect your reputation and the reputation of the trademark you are marketing.
If you want to achieve efficient multiple repetitions, you need to develop a system. Every system, or better said process, has cornerstones that I like to call steps. I call them steps because sales can only happen when we're active. Active means movement.

The naked truth: An example of sales steps

The customer is engrossed in reading your quote while constantly complaining and moaning: Encourage them: "Excuse me, I have a feeling I haven't explained some things well enough. Could you tell me which details you would like me to explain some more?"
You could see this as leading the client. In part that's exactly what you're doing since even if they reply "No", it's not about the wrong answer. Perhaps you're dealing with the wrong client but haven't noticed it yet. Perhaps you were too aggressive and the client was unable to express their expectations. Life is dynamic and sometimes we enter a curve too quickly and can drift a little. The most important thing is to learn from your mistakes, gain new experiences and share them with your colleagues so that you are all even more successful tomorrow.

5.4 THE SALES CYCLE IN STEPS

Sales steps always happen in practice. In reality, some steps can happen in a very short period of time or concurrently. An analysis is an overview of the situation, which is important in increasing a salesperson's confidence, since they know who and how they can help. We're often not aware of analysis as we do it spontaneously. For example, if you enter a room, you analyse the situation without realising it and move toward your intended place, or you sit down on a chair not on the floor next to the chair. It's similar in the business world and sales. The next step, called implementation, is the clear direction and activity that you need to carry out to achieve your goal. You can see it as choosing one of many steps in the direction of your final goal. Parallel to implementation, activities are formed into tested tools that are important for subsequent work (5 question tool).

In the long run, success is connected to experiences we have encountered in our work. Of course, we avoid bad ones. It's important to hold on to successful activities for all future sales events as this is how we achieve repetition.

Every effective training session is followed by results. In sales steps, this is called building skills. The potential customer, who we want to turn into our buyer, has to feel comfortable and safe in our company and with our solution. Details make the difference between successful and very successful salespeople. That's why this step is vital for successful business and the salesperson's well-being.

A successful entrepreneur or salesperson is a long time in the making. During this time we acquire many habits and bad habits. A habit is a useful activity or skill that we use in our business. And a bad habit is something "bad" people acquire as a shortcut in business events. We already talked about them in the chapter on the basics of sales. Not everyone is your buyer, that's why you need to select suitable buyers by using the right commercial philosophy. Even though we've covered this topic already, it's important to emphasise it as it's one of the foundations of sales.

It's important to let customers find out on their own through the sales steps why they should listen to us and what makes us stand out from other providers. The next step is opportunity -the moment when the client learns about the solution they've been looking for and makes direct contact with us. Be well-prepared for a sales pitch since you'll have very little time to talk about your activities and the benefits to your buyers. Continue by asking the right questions. It's not always answers that are important, but the client's thinking about the problems for which you offer a solution. Make a summary that will help you prepare a suitable solution. The customer must gain trust in you, meaning you're

Sales Closing

the right person to solve their problem. By presenting the quote you can strengthen their opinion that you're the right choice. The quote solves a concrete problem or pain described by the customer and is also attractive in economic terms. The next important step is to step back a little and encourage the customer to think things through and make the right decision. This is how you create an advantage, as you're not putting any pressure on the customer. The customer mustn't feel forced to buy, instead feeling that this is the last chance for them to resolve the problem with the right business partner. A quality conversation is a way of rejecting objections, which usually don't arise if the presentation is well-prepared. We've now come to closing the sale, i.e. the administrative-operational work (signing the contract and issuing the invoice) as the sale was successful. The goal is to establish the level of satisfaction of the buyer, who will recommend you further and indirectly help you find new customers provided the after-sales support is sufficient.

The cycle is completed by continuously repeating itself and rotating - this is how we can build a successful business story in the long run.

The sales steps cycle is a way of reaching the next highest level in the sales business. Usually, salespeople decide to think about this only once things aren't going as planned or when they start to feel like they don't know how to sell. I often meet excellent salespeople who've given up, even though they're so close to making it and having a great career. I would therefore like to finish the sales steps section with a recommendation.

If your sales cycle has stopped, seek external help from a coach or mentor. It's such a shame to give up just before life rewards you with the fruits of your hard work.

Developing a salesperson is work that is never really finished. A salesperson is someone who gains new experiences and new knowledge every day and, through that, opportunities for progress that never end.

Mind map 12: Sales steps

Sales cycle

The cycle is completed and can rotate; we start each cycle at the beginning and try to improve the details to perfection, in the sense of successfully closing sales.

These steps are:
- analysis,
- implementation,
- repetition,
- skills,
- habits,
- "let's start again".

5.5 PRACTICAL PART: SALES CLOSING

Task 1: *With a partner think of a sales situation and determine if your partner is the right buyer.*

Task 2: *Find your buyer's pain and write down five objections the buyer has.*

Task 3: *Define a quality conversation for the given sales situation in a few sentences.*

Task 4: *With the help of the sales cycle, prepare a sales closing for the given sales situation using the suggested steps.*

Task 5: *Prepare a sales cycle for selling your favourite vegetable and your favourite clothing service.*

Task 6: *Try to determine the buyer's satisfaction level for the given sales situation.*

Task 7: *Write down what else you can do for your buyer's satisfaction.*

5.6 IN BRIEF: SALES CLOSING

1. When it comes to sales, practice is most important.
2. To be able to successfully close a sale, you need to observe the client well.
3. While talking to them, you need to adapt to your client.
4. When opening their "pain" you should do so with a pre-prepared plan, which includes sales closings.
5. Try to control your "sales price complex".
6. Prepare well for any objections in your closing talks.
7. Your motto and your principle should always be - Sales isn't a scam but help.
8. Remember - closing the sale is the most important part. Everything else isn't as important.
9. Follow the sales steps in the sales cycle.

6. CROSS-SELLING

6.1 WHAT IS CROSS-SELLING?

Cross-selling is one of the most demanding sales in the business world, even if seemingly simple at first glance. It's divided into two segments:

1. Attracting customers, which is done by marketing and sales methods we have already discussed.
2. Successful and repeatable sales.

Both segments are similar; the difference is that the second segment includes a part that focuses on selling to existing buyers and is an upgrade on the first one. This means more can be sold with it or the product range can be expanded. To sell more to an existing buyer doesn't mean pressuring the buyer in the sense of "Come on, buy, buy" or similar manipulations. The salesperson's intention is to get the existing buyer to buy a wider range of products, i.e. getting them to buy things they usually buy from other suppliers. The challenge we take on in this case is to ensure added value - to make it worth the buyer buying from us. Retaining the buyer's positive feelings is the most difficult and risky part. The buyer shouldn't feel "deceived". A good salesperson always presents the reasons for related sales as if they're thinking like a buyer. They need to be able to explain to themselves and the buyer why it is worthwhile buying from them and what will they gain by doing so.

6.2 DON'T SELL, ADVISE

Cross-selling activities are a business opportunity, not "begging"; you should therefore see them as something extremely positive. I don't need to point out that it's much easier to sell to an existing customer than find a new one. I call the method that I've found to be most effective in practice "an approach through the added value view". This means: if a buyer buys a machine from you and consumable goods from another provider, they decide to buy the latter from you as well. You can achieve this by presenting their decision as a technological issue, since your machinery works best with your materials. As a salesperson you cannot make the decision for the buyer, but you are also to blame if the buyer opts for a similar but inferior material because of the lower price. This can jeopardise your technological solution as results become average or even unacceptable. In the end this means the buyer spent the money and now the solution isn't working properly. You should present added value using the buyer's example and evaluate every detail. I won't deny that some salespeople exaggerate, but I advise against this since statistical and measured data always tells the truth. This is why in cross-selling you need to prepare exceptionally well for meetings and all other sales events.

So, cross-selling is sales activities with which you sell a larger amount or an updated solution that you have in your wider range to an existing buyer. This means contacting a buyer who already trusts you and doesn't need further proof of the quality of your solutions since they are already a satisfied user of one of your solutions or products. In marketing jargon, this kind of quote is often called "all-in-one-place", which means exactly that: a firm bond between the buyer and your company. Usually, things aren't as simple as described above.

The relationship in cross-selling could be compared to other interpersonal relationships. You need to work on it constantly and prove that your intentions are genuine and directed towards helping others.
This is why I tell all salespeople not to sell to the existing buyer, but to advise the existing buyer. If your buyer's issue falls within an area not covered by your company's solutions, you can genuinely advise them who to trust. This way you will further enhance the bond you have with your business partner.

I recommend that you don't hide your problems from "good" people as you never know who might offer you good advice. I have had many positive experiences. I once had a specific health challenge that I didn't hide and was actively seeking a solution for. While enjoying lunch and coffee in a relaxing atmosphere, I enquired about hospitals in foreign countries and experts in this particular health area. I will never forget a lady from a distinguished foreign company who mentioned the name of a hospital and a doctor whose name I didn't recognise, but who was one of the world's leading experts in his field. I called the hospital and visited the doctor. While searching for a solution, we developed a genuine relationship. I'm happy to say that everyone who I've politely asked for advice has reacted positively. This goes for personal as well as business questions.

The naked truth: An example of giving advice

When giving advice to your partners in cross-selling, you shouldn't act the "wise-guy"; instead, your advice should be well-founded and relevant to the solution that will bring your buyer additional savings or earnings.
An example of a good piece of advice could be: "Mr. Smith, if you use our lubricants, your machines will work twice as long and more efficiently. This means the 20% higher cost of the lubricant will be covered

by lower repair costs and you will get more for your money, which means you will save even more."
Cross-selling that is not well-founded usually doesn't go down very well:
"Smith, if you use our lubricant, the machine will work like clockwork..."

6.3 FORCING THE BUYER

The biggest mistake you can make, which can even lead to losing a buyer forever, is forcing the buyer, even though you know your solution isn't the best. Forcing the buyer can be as simple as the wrong approach or non-verbal communication. Even by bringing the buyer an excessive gift before any deal has been made.
It takes a long time to build a good name. But you can squander it in a moment. Moments change our lives, whether they're happy or unhappy. But those which we can save and keep uncomplicated using our reason, will forever remain on the list of our achievements.
Remember, having a sense for just the right amount of force is a talent; but you can also learn it by following the advice covered in the chapter on the salesperson's characteristics.

The naked truth: Examples of forcing the buyer in a given sales situation

Forcing the buyer can be recognised quickly. If you're the buyer, don't tolerate it; as the salesperson you should never use it.
There are many ways of forcing the buyer:
- By using sentences like: "Buy it, you'll see that you'll like it; your neighbour also bought it. What's 50 Euros to you? You can't live without this product any longer!"
- By using touches: This is usually a kind of seduction.

- By making threats and insults: "OK, if you're so smart, I'll ask the director! I'll call the management!"

6.4 CROSS-SELLING MEANS TRUSTING YOURSELF AND THE SOLUTION YOU ARE SELLING

Believing in your product or solution is the precondition you convey in your contact with a potential buyer. If you have doubts about your solution, product or sales price, you'll unintentionally show it and your buyers will notice it. This mistake often happens even before you've launched the solution and started marketing it. If you didn't participate in the development of the solution and are only in charge of marketing, your colleague has made this mistake since they didn't hand over this part very professionally. This means, you weren't convinced and wowed by the solution.

Someone who presents their solution without radiating any positive energy and is only acting makes mistakes which are very revealing.

You can avoid this issue by asking questions. A motivated person who wishes to succeed as a salesperson wants to know everything. This is especially important in cross-selling. A trained person who hands the solution over to a salesperson within the company knows very well that they need to "sell" the salesperson the solution, since this is the only way they'll be able to market it successfully.

Cross-selling means trusting the trademark and the company marketing it, and realising that you're truly helping your buyers to a more successful and better life. Every modern company invests in the technical or sales development of their solutions. That's why buyers can expect many new solutions that will make their lives easier in the future as well.

A typical mistake that technically advanced companies make (and which is reflected in calm sales results) is a product that is "too good" and has difficulties accepting a competitive new generation model.

6.5 CROSS-SELLING SUPPLEMENTS THE SALESPERSON'S PROMISES

Cross-selling must supplement the promises the salesperson previously made about solving the buyer's problem.

Companies with poor after-sales support and poor customer service lose loyal customers in the long run. Making credible and realistic promises is a big challenge for the modern salesperson. It often happens that a competitor offers something we can't, and under pressure we promise the same. Of course, the buyer expects to get what the salesperson promised. If the promise we made isn't in line with the company's policy, we're bound to get into trouble as the buyers will ask about it.
To avoid such situations, you should forward the information to your company and find a solution in a meeting with your colleagues. Clever companies often use "tricks" to make something that is self-evident seem like a concrete solution. That's why you need to study the information you received and not rush to conclusions.

Buyers want the fastest, the best and the cheapest solutions. Even though these three are mutually exclusive, the modern world's tempo demands them. Innovation and innovative methods often change the dimensions of established practices. I often advise entrepreneurs to think back, starting with the sales price of competitive solutions and then going all the way back along their process to the production price, discount value, marketing etc. The best innovations can occur when the calculation doesn't add up. For example, simplifying the implementation process often also means easier maintenance.

6.6 AFTER-SALES SUPPORT

When we think of after-sales support we think of maintenance or servicing. But it includes much more and is closely connected with cross-selling. It also includes notifying buyers of preventative maintenance checks, innovations, details etc. When it comes to after-sales support, we act similarly to when selling complex solutions, where we give the customer time to think about the more complex quote and carry out a follow up. The day before visiting the buyer you should call them and make an appointment in case there have been any changes to their schedule. You should also inform them about what to expect. You need to prepare well for your phone call and make a list of words that you should say in a particular order. You must think I'm complicating things. But, clearly saying certain words in a process that is equally clear and logical to the client is a sign of professionalism that will boost the buyer's confidence in the company, trademark and the person calling them.

The naked truth: An example of after-sales support

"Hi, Mr. Monday, I'm calling from Solution Inc. Peter speaking. I'm calling about assembling the packing line robot. I've been informed that the equipment is ready, and would like to know if we can assemble it in your production hall as agreed? Agreed, Mr. Monday. We will only need a forklift to unload the equipment from our lorry. It'll take about five minutes to do so. After that, my colleague and I will carry out the assembly. We expect to finish the assembly on Wednesday morning.

Would it be possible to carry out the operator training right after that? We'd like to monitor the operations on your line for one more shift to remedy any deficiencies that might appear if mistakes are made during use. So, could we do that on Friday? If you have any further questions or needs, we can talk about them on the spot in the next few days while I'm visiting you." You can also add a question for an additional order or cross-selling.

The phone call is very sales oriented - as is appropriate for a modern company You called the buyer to discuss the assembly - this is reassuring for the buyer. But not only that - subconsciously they sense that they're dealing with a well-organised and professional team. They are aware of the steps required and therefore don't think the assembly will take too long, leaving them satisfied. There were no hesitations or unrelated sentences in the phone call, which shows how important preparation for the phone call is. Peter also reminded the buyer that he would be at their company for a few days and that they could come to him if they had any further questions or needs.

6.7 PRACTICAL PART: CROSS-SELLING

Task 1: *Use cross-selling methods to introduce additional sales opportunities in the given solution or product.*

Task 2: *Try to win over the buyer's trust for the given sales situation and advise them in their further decisions.*

Task 3: *Try to force your solutions for the given sales situation to your partner and then observe their reaction.*

Task 4: *Introduce after-sales support in the selected sales situation.*

6.8 IN BRIEF: CROSS-SELLING

People buy feelings and stories; that's why cross-selling is very important for happy endings to business stories. Well prepared cross-selling means good after-sales support that is often worth more than the best price. You could compare cross-selling to salt with your meal. Just a pinch of it will change the dish and, thereby, also your meal.

1. Cross-selling is one of the most demanding sales.
2. Cross-selling is giving advice.
3. Avoid forcing your buyer.
4. Cross-selling supplements the salesperson's promises.

7. YOU CAN'T DO IT ALL ON YOUR OWN

While reading this book you may have noticed that I like to point out that a company is its people: the management and every employee. This sentence might seem obvious, but it happens way too often that a company's owners and managing directors want to do everything on their own while treating their employees as an "extension" of their left hand.
We often don't realise that we simply can't do it all on our own. In a physical and an intellectual sense.

7.1 TIME

The only thing that is divided fairly in this world is time. We all have 24 hours a day. The founders and owners of smaller companies, who are used to entrepreneurial ways of operating, often turn out to be the biggest clogs for further development. 100% control of every event in a company is beyond the temporal boundaries of one person and can lead to activities that are essential for the company being delayed.

Company culture is created by management and then transferred to co-workers. Suitable behaviour, respecting people's values and monitoring the tasks performed is a reflection of management. Employees can come to work to earn their salary, or they can do their job with a personal mission, which takes the company to a higher level.

People are emotional creatures with personal values

and their own behavioural patterns ingrained by their childhood home and surroundings. Due to our past experiences and the combination of different cultures we're exposed to, we are also defined by our beliefs, which put us in different dimensions of life without even realising it.

7.2 SALES PROCESSES AND WORK DISTRIBUTION

As you've learned by now, sales processes are the most important part of sales. In addition to their time management and professional planning, suitable work distribution is also essential.

You cannot skip sales processes, but that doesn't mean that you can exceed the deadline you've set. The number of activities happening in a certain stage of the sales cycle can also be a problem. Such and other similar issues can be resolved by simply distributing the work correctly. While doing so, you should make sure everyone participating in these sales activities is informed.

Sales processes can be divided into:

- Marketing part: attracting prospects, finding out who else might be interested in the solution.
- Professional part: determining challenges and issues, finding solutions and confirmation that the solution is suitable.
- Sales part: summary of challenges, solutions and sales closings.

7.3 DEVELOPMENT OF THE SALES DEPARTMENT

As with a company, a sales department develops gradually. For every construction project you need good materials - and to build a good sales department you need good salespeople. You can find and select them on the basis of their references, knowledge, skills and talents.

Knowledge and skills can be quickly supplemented through mentorship by the main salesperson or head of sales, especially if the sales team is made up of young and enthusiastic people.

The most important thing when it comes to the development of the sales department is the salespeople's attitude to sales problems and their personal mission. The company management and the head of sales are responsible for that.

The biggest challenge for a good sales department is creating and handling activities that are required. Updated activities are very important to make sure that the competition doesn't get ahead. So, for the correct distribution of work you need to correctly distribute sales activities in terms of time as well as the individuals in the sales team.

7.4 LEADERSHIP

Leadership is one of the essential skills needed to be an entrepreneur. In part it's a talent as it covers a specific "people-sense", but the larger part of it is a skill that can be learned. Learned over time, not over night. This means it requires certain experience.

Leadership is done by people, which means the same characteristics listed in the chapter on the features of a good salesperson and entrepreneur in general apply to a manager as well. The most difficult task for a leader is to assign employees to the right job functions to ensure operations run smoothly.

Leaders often forget that some people can do their work satisfactorily, but suffer from human characteristics while doing so. A good leader should notice this and take action. Common practice in such cases is to rotate employees in their job functions or workplaces.
Successful companies do this for many reasons. This is not so common in smaller companies. Mainly because employee qualifications and skills are very varied - the managing director simply cannot afford to have more people with the same profile. A solution to this, which usually everyone finds suitable, but unfortunately isn't so in practice, is precisely determined work processes. A job function has its responsibilities and work processes, which result in well performed work and satisfied buyers who pay you for this work. That is by buying your excellent solutions and products.

What is leadership

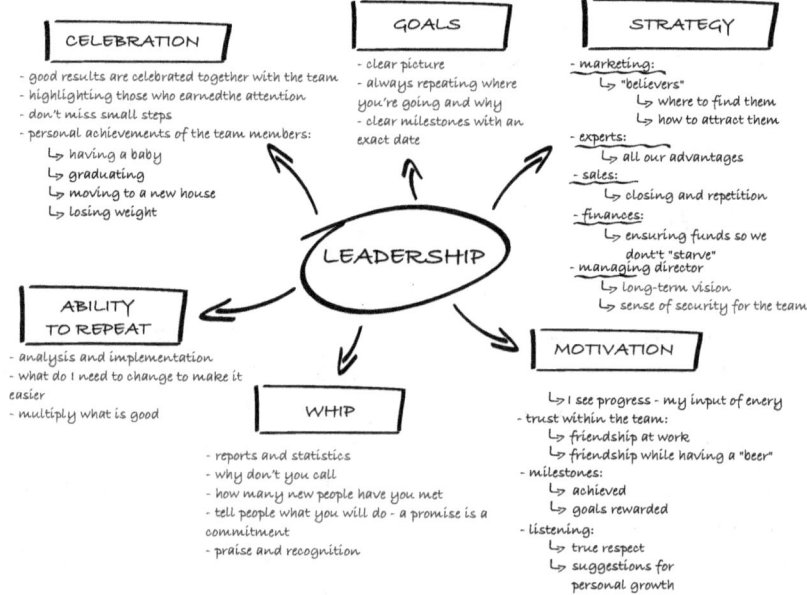

Mind map 13: Leadership

Leadership can also be compared to the basic order in the animal world. A leader is a person at the front of the pack who is able to convince their pack to follow them towards the goals, direction and strategy for common success. Motivation is the key leadership segment. Unmotivated people cannot be led - this usually results in very poor results, in terms of the team's achievements and the company as a whole.

In addition to the usual work problems, a leader also faces the problems of leading people and, with that, the problems of everyone who's in the team.

Unfortunately leaders cannot easily transfer the skills presented in a job well-performed to other or new employees. An external observer, e.g. an adviser or an ISO auditor, might wonder how come a company doesn't have a system to do so in place. More often than not, the answer is the same. The company slowly grew from a one-person company to a company with several employees. At the beginning, the owner is also the director who is unaware of their tasks. They also work as the mentor to every new employee. Eventually, as the company grows, they have too many tasks. Someone who's built their company from scratch and has led it to a medium-sized company finds this the hardest. They simply cannot learn how to hand over the reins and entrust their colleagues with decisive tasks. They become a control freak, who is constantly looking over other people's shoulders and gets nervous if others achieve the same result using a different, perhaps even better, path, since things weren't done the way they had imagined them.

This is usually a big hindrance to the company's further development. In practice, such people usually don't see their mistakes as they find it difficult to admit they exist. Entrepreneurs, who are very passionate people, have difficulties accepting obvious facts when other people or colleagues point them out. But, usually, when they address the issues directly, they bring about changes that are just as successful as the business they are running. Parallel to this many other things happen that aren't noticed by everyone. The "boss" also imparts the company's business or commercial philosophy to each new employee. It often happens that the first employees stay at the company the longest - this is because they want to grow with the company and also understand the goals that the company wants to achieve. Once the company's growth "explodes", due to market requirements or increased demand, the mentorship system is cast aside as there's simply not enough time or neglected due to work-overload. The main leader doesn't have time to induct the new employees; they are "thrown" among unwritten processes and left to figure it out on their own. Since people are different and have different values, some just can't deal with such a "shock" very well; this leads to their work being full of mistakes and them feeling unhappy. The end result of inefficient processes and management is employees leaving the company. An efficient solution to this problem is internal seminars to introduce new employees to the company and a mentorship programme, wherein "masters", skilled in certain tasks, are activated as new mentors to pass on their special knowledge to new colleagues. A double effect is achieved, which is practically and economically most favourable for the company. The right employees remain at the company for a long time, and those who cannot accept the company's philosophy look for a new career path, which is certainly the best solution for them and the company.

The processes in sales are as precisely defined as those on the production line. Even though intuition and improvisation are more present in sales, business processes are always running in the background. Excellent salespeople are, of course, those who are also talented in addition to knowing the processes. This means that they spontaneously react to a sales situation and, therefore, cannot "accept the fact" that sales is also a theoretical process. External experts, advisers and coaches often analyse such people. A good salesperson can be analysed up to a certain point, and their steps written down as theory in order to transfer best practice to other employees. In practice such salespeople are worried about sharing their know-how as they think they might get replaced. When presenting information or running a sales meeting it isn't just about the words the salesperson says. Non-verbal communication, posture, and tone of voice are very important – all of which are hard to define within a process. In my opinion only a top theatre actor can "copy" an excellent salesperson.

There's a principle in sales: "If you can't measure it, it doesn't exist." After you've mastered the processes or sales steps, you need to prepare a policy for managing your daily activities and short-term directions.

You've probably realised that salespeople have to excel at all kinds of communication since this is our largest and most commonly used tool. A salesperson has to explain to a potential buyer in just a few sentences what the advantages of the solution they are offering are. So, it's not about lies and such, but it's simply the case that the potential buyer won't buy the solution unless they know all the facts. Due to their ability to "operate" with words I recommend that salespeople only use numbers in their daily reports.

It's crucial to start preparing employees for leadership positions early on through a mentorship programme. It's best to become a leader before you're responsible for a group of people – far better than learning how to do it in practice with irreparable consequences.

Five-level leadership

Many theories have been written about five-level leadership, and many are also true in practice. I'd like to share with you a principle I use at work and pass on to my clients - who usually attest to its effectiveness.
In this case it's not just about transferring responsibility from the mentor to the trainee. There's also a parallel effect - the expert gets to refine their practices by analysing the trainee's actions and learning process.
The five-level mentorship system consists of:

1. I do my work independently (I'm skilled at my work).
2. I'm working and a new colleague is learning from me and is helping me (mentorship).
3. The new colleague is working and I'm their mentor.
4. The new colleague is working independently (they have become skilled).
5. The new colleague is teaching someone else from the company (has become the mentor).

"Ageing" of the salesforce is also something that needs to be considered in a sales team. People are a company's biggest capital, and you don't want to needlessly lose them. Advice from someone who's already been in a battle fought by a younger colleague can be priceless.
A good head of sales has a well-developed method of observation, suggesting help and practical presentation, which pushes the whole team forwards to new victories. Sales supervision is done by constant numerical evaluation and a logical vision for the future.
Salespeople are people of fantasies and open debate; that's why their reporting to the head of sales should be limited to concrete numbers: the number of phone calls made, number of meetings held, number of successful closings and total sales amounts. If you tell your

salespeople to inform you "in words and pictures", as I like to joke, you'll receive a novel in your inbox every day.

Is leadership a mistake

Leadership in the sense of military leadership is outdated in the modern world. But in the precise plan of business processes, the personal responsibility of the individual exceeds the need for leadership on the personal level. A leader who can present direction and goals well can achieve unsurpassable results with a responsible and professional team.

The question "Is leadership a mistake?" most often occurs when one of the employees from the same level is promoted. This means that the employee promoted to head of the team or department experiences a "leadership christening" by their colleagues. At that time, good organisation within the company is crucial as the immediate leader can influence the stimulative pay or salary of each individual by using evaluation forms. This means that they take over leading their colleagues softly through their integrity and authority. Pre-preparation is also important in such cases, something I encourage very strongly. Enough leaders have to be trained to keep stock. Of course, a lot depends on the motive that the individual has at that particular moment in their life. If they are highly skilled as a mentor, are able to define tasks clearly and stick to agreements as a person with strong integrity does, this is one of the best guides for business life. The easiest way to train a stock of leaders is by assigning them individual tasks. This means that the leader hands over a task to an individual and assigns a third employee to help them carry it out. This way the individual learns about the weight of responsibility for the entrusted task and at the same time motivates the colleague to perform the task quickly and successfully.

Leadership can never be a mistake, since the modern market's complexity and demands are the criteria that expect high-quality solutions with the optimal use of funds; we can only achieve this by efficiently managing business functions.

Leadership in practice

As already mentioned, mentorship is one of the most important advantages that can benefit a company and the individual greatly. In the olden days it was master craftsmen who taught their apprentices a certain craft, and the latter never forgot them even when they themselves became masters; similar is true today. When it comes to leadership, it is very lucky and important to be surrounded by experts at the beginning of your business career. This is how to gain the most knowledge and skills that will benefit you in your life. Plenty of knowledge remains in each of us who have had several mentors in our lives - knowledge that is still useful in our business lives today. Each of us also has their own faults, which we stubbornly keep until we've experienced a strong enough "pain" that motivates us to learn new, better habits. The biggest mentors in my life were the people who let me observe their mistakes and knew how to say "Sorry" to the client and remedy their mistakes.

Some people see leadership and management as rising above other people, losing friends or dulling the social feeling. It's definitely not about that. We know that a ship can't sail in three directions at the same time, that's why it only has one captain. Leadership is not only a skill, it also demands understanding fellow humans and being self-critical of your managerial orders.

Who am I? Where do I want to get to? What is my mission? These are just a few questions many people dislike or refuse to hear. Answers to such questions evoke strong responsibility, and if we say them out loud also a serious commitment. Complete integrity is good for a leader's conscience and a long life.

The most common mistake leaders make is losing interpersonal sincerity. I can't generalise this claim, but I can incite a moment for deliberation within you: "Do you greet and praise each colleague individually when you enter the company premises in the morning?" It will only take you a few seconds with each colleague for this powerful motivational gesture. If other co-workers hear the praise, the praised person will remain motivated for longer. Of course, all of this is only true if you're a charismatic leader who keeps their word, listens to ideas and gives out the right advice to their co-workers. If not, this might even undermine you. Adaptability is the "source of life". Adapting to a given situation is an ability all living things have: plants, animals and people. We're born with talents, but in order to survive we also need habits, techniques and experiences. No leopard cub knows how to kill an impala, even though its instinct tells it to grab it by the throat. The same is true for the skill of leadership.

There are quite a few techniques and skills that are important to a leader's "survival". The most important ones are basic human values: integrity, family, work, respect others etc. A good leader has to learn a few important habits:

- Become a good listener.
- Attentively observe people around them.
- Become a good advisor with full empathy.
- Dare to help co-workers in all areas of life, in their business and private lives.
- Give their co-workers a reason to be appreciated due to the high added value they create together with the other employees of the

company.

You've become a successful entrepreneur when your role model sees you as competition.

At a certain stage in their personal development all people look for a role model who they believe is living the life and doing the work they too find good and interesting. By expanding in your field you can become a serious competitor to your role model. This is a sign that you've really worked hard and have become a success in your business.

7.5 BOARD MEETING AND MEETING

The easiest way to implement and control leadership is at meetings and board meetings. Meetings and board meetings are important for maintaining control over sales and other activities in a company.

What is a meeting and what is a board meeting

There is an obvious difference between a meeting and a board meeting.
Since there are many available resources that explain what a meeting is, we'll mention it only briefly. A meeting is a gathering of people from different companies or the same one intended for open communication with a pre-determined topic. It's led by a formal or informal leader. This is the person who organised the meeting. There are different types of meetings: informing, decision-making, problem-solving (challenge-solving if using sales jargon), creating group affiliation, brainstorming etc. It's important to prepare for meetings and that their duration is limited in time. If they are overly long, they can result in poor conclusions as the point of the meeting usually "eludes" the participants.

Unlike a meeting, a board meeting is intended for efficient decision-making by the manager or the management team. It's conducted by the company's managing director or the person who is responsible for all the decisions adopted. Thorough preparation is thus important and all participants must be well-informed about the agenda. A board meeting is intended for decision-making, not informing. Informing is done before the board meeting is held. That's why a board meeting is usually a brief event with several conclusions and short discussions.

Why is a board meeting important for the company

Let's ask ourselves, who is the board meeting more important for - the participants or the company? Since we know that a company without employees is like a "haunted house", we can conclude that a board meeting is very important for the participants of the board meeting as well as for the business the company is involved in and, consequently, also for its buyers on the market.
Technical drawings are very clear. Their expertise is composed of different implementation processes that lead us to the end result of the service or product. Managing a company is a much more complex, planned structure. It's much easier to determine the vision, goals and strategy if we have an insight into the short-term past. If so, planning can be done well. But, it's always difficult to foresee what the company's direction will be as environmental, human, political and other changes can force the head of the company to find a different path; one that will take the business in another, even if still planned, direction.

Important decisions are made at board meetings and that's why it's essential to the managing director's or company president's decision-making process.
If an addition by one of the participants is judged to be too complex at the board meeting, it is the purpose

of the board meeting to ask the initiator to thoroughly prepare the materials that must be sent by a certain date to all board meeting participants. The chairperson than calls an extraordinary board meeting with a precise date.

The naked truth: An example of an invitation to a board meeting

The best invitation to a board meeting are the minutes from the previous board meeting, which means the board meeting participants have to prepare and provide answers in their field of expertise. Good preparation for a board meeting, in the sense of discussing open issues, is important. Complex and demanding issues have to be discussed in a separate meeting held for the essential participants; that's why we present the time and date, reasons and the meeting participants at a board meeting. A board meeting with five participants can take about thirty minutes, which is enough to decide on the issues listed in the invitation. Board meetings that take too long not only waste time, but are also de-motivational. As a rule, you can use the following example:

Dear board meeting participants,
I'd like to invite you to the management board meeting on Tuesday 2nd February XXXX at 11 am in meeting room A with the following agenda. A confirmation of manager reports for their responsible areas:

- *Fulfilment of production implementation plan (report in figures and enclosed PDF diagrams) - 5-minute explanation by managing director John Monday.*
- *Sales plan and open opportunities (report in figures and enclosed PDF diagrams) - 5-minute explanation by Melissa Tuesday.*
- *Marketing activities and success statistics for the last campaign (report in figures and enclosed PDF*

diagrams) -
  5-minute explanation by Melissa Tuesday.
- *Cash flow statement (report in figures and enclosed PDF diagrams) - 5-minute explanation by Melissa Tuesday.*
- *Financial plan and borrowing per project (report in figures and enclosed PDF diagrams) - 5-minute explanation by Irene Wednesday.*
- *Open HR notices and introduction of new colleagues (report in figures and enclosed PDF diagrams) - 5-minute explanation by Anne Friday.*
- *Working group determination and voting for the new XXX investment - a three member team will be selected, one of the members will also serve as the president (10 minutes).*
- *Member applications accepted until 10 a.m. Tuesday, 2nd February.*
- *Selecting and approving a coaching provider as proposed by HR (Anne Friday) - estimated budget EUR 18,000 (10 minutes).*
- *Research and development, two people (quotes enclosed).*
- *Selling in foreign markets, two people (quotes enclosed).*

The board meeting will take an hour and fifteen minutes so please plan other obligations after 12.15 p.m. I expect you to be well-prepared and informed about the proposed topics to enable an efficient decision-making process.
Sincerely, (SIGNATURE)

Presiding over a board meeting

You can figure out the important facts you should follow in order to ensure efficient board meeting conclusions from the examples. Presiding over a board meeting can be defined by rules or you can see it as a meeting of internal decision-makers who decide what will be done.

Presiding over a board meeting following a process

Presiding over a board meeting can follow a process similar to the one below:

1. Congratulating the chairperson for certain achievements.
2. Expressing worries if some things haven't gone as planned since the previous board meeting.
3. Seeing if anyone is holding a grudge and attempting to set the future direction - grudges should be resolved individually and not at a board meeting.
4. Open point, no discussion.
5. Proposing solutions.
6. Voting and deciding.
7. Reaching decisions.
8. Setting milestones.
9. Conclusion and invitation to the next board meeting.

A good leader doesn't attempt to motivate their colleagues at a board meeting, but makes sure that they come to the board meeting well-prepared and motivated.

The naked truth: An example of presiding over a board meeting

When presiding over a board meeting, you can use the following sentences.
1. At the start: "Thank you for coming."
2. At the beginning of discussing the agenda: "Has anyone not read the agenda and points for discussion?"
3. If anything goes wrong: "Dear colleague, I'm

afraid I must ask you to leave the meeting!"
4. If you wish to emphasise something: "As regards points four and five, this decision was taken by me and I ask you to respect it."
5. When making conclusions: "I kindly ask you to respect the conclusions made."

An example of a conclusion and entry in the minutes. "Melissa Tuesday explained to us that last month's decline in sales was a consequence of our buyer's XXX problems. We've adopted a measure for them to prepare a solution for their clients in the field of XYZ together with the development department. After this, we will visit 50 potential clients from our database and test the new solution in practice. We have to compose a team of sales and technical experts and prepare a suitable quote by 10th February XXXX. The sales activities of visiting customers and presentations will be completed by 15th March XXXX. Following this, we can expect revenue by the end of September this year.
"Would anyone like to add anything?"
"I suggest that Melissa keeps us informed of the project's progress with figures and diagrams every Friday by 2 p.m. Melissa, since you've highlighted the seriousness of the given situation, we wish to include all the board meeting participants to ensure the acquisition of new buyers, i.e. to join forces.

In the example, the board meeting chairperson's words have set a few recognisable tools. You should never descend to the level of creating artificial panic or insults and personal disqualification.

1. You ask questions, even though the report contains numbers, so that all the decision-makers are aware of the seriousness of the problem.
2. If you're experiencing difficulties in one area,

set up a micro planning and evaluating system (very precise).
3. It's important to call on the participants so that they are ready for the next activities.

This means: ask questions whose replies you're expecting. When stated in public, these answers become a commitment of those who said them. We also know that a person with integrity doesn't just say anything, but assumes full responsibility for the things that they said.

Common mistakes in presiding over a board meeting

Mistakes at board meetings happen mainly because the chairperson allows them to.
What shouldn't be allowed:
1. Straying from the subject of discussion - this often shows that participant hasn't prepared very well and they're trying to divert attention.
2. Most participants agree with one of the "powerful" people to avoid being held personally responsible.
3. "Wise people's" lectures to teach responsible participants a lesson waste time and energy. They usually comment on a field or project that they don't know well-enough.
4. A conclusion can't be drawn as materials haven't been well-enough prepared for the participants to be able to make a decision.
The chairperson is at fault in part since poorly prepared materials shouldn't be included on the agenda.
5. Participants fail to prepare reports and threaten the next board meeting and business operations in general.

Usually, reports shouldn't be longer than one page.

Efficiency can be achieved through decision-making based on statistically clear data without subjective opinions. To ensure better understanding and that guidelines for the future are followed, responsible managers have 5 minutes to convince the board meeting participants to support them in their future work.

The naked truth: Examples of common mistakes in presiding over a board meeting

- Participants allow the "old hand" to take the initiative, whereby they get the "nodders" to follow their strong voice, authority and speaking abilities.
- Participants "berate" other participants or criticise them inappropriately.
- The chairperson is too quiet and is drowned out.
- Someone is typing on their mobile phone.
- Someone hasn't said a word during the entire board meeting - they're not really there.
- The minute taker adapts the conclusions to their interests; they should read each conclusion aloud.

Solutions to the mistakes in presiding over a board meeting

Setting a seating plan is an important part of preparing for a board-meeting. The best seating arrangement for a board meeting is a round table since everyone can see each other directly. If this isn't possible, a slightly wider rectangular table is also effective. It's the chairperson's task to seat participants in accordance with the relationships within the company. If two participants don't get along very well, they should sit next to each other and not at opposite ends. This way they are seated in the same way as behind a negotiating table, which makes the dynamic discussion of opposing views more effective.

Board meeting participants should stick to the following

unwritten rules:

- Suitable clothes, in line with the company's culture. This refers to expressing equality among participants, since any deviation could seem to be a sign of superiority.
- The pitch and tone of voice should be appropriate. Choleric outbursts don't belong in such meetings as participants have to make their decisions responsibly without egocentric or other emotional outbursts.
- No mobile phones or other similar "disturbers" should be allowed. Interactive content should be presented on a big screen or projector. Those who are prepared for the board meeting don't need additional information on their devices.
- Participants should stick to the topic of discussion. Board meetings often take too long because of one simple reason. If the business in one of the areas of discussion isn't doing well, the person responsible for that area might feel under attack. This is how the topic is lost. When people at board meetings feel threatened, they react in different ways:
- The most common reaction is to divert attention to someone or something else; by doing this everyone else's thoughts are also directed away and the topic is lost.
- Some become aggressive and insulting and even resort to violence towards other participants. That's why the chairperson's main duty is to never allow this, especially by never allowing diversion away from the board meeting's common thread.
- Participants should encourage debate. Someone who isn't an important decision-maker cannot attend a board meeting. Usually, only the key and most important people from the company

are present at board meetings. The chairperson must ensure that nobody remains quiet for the entire board meeting, only voicing an opinion when voting to accept or reject a decision. The chairperson should refrain from "supporter" reactions until the last opinion has been expressed before a conclusion is made. This way they'll encourage participants that it's acceptable to say "NO" and show them that all opinions count. If not, some company "soldiers" may end up only nodding in order to please the managing director and not expressing their opinion, which doesn't bring any added value.

- The chairperson should preside over the meeting in the following way: "John, I know you're the expert in the field of production; however, I'd like to know what you think of this XYZ? The chairperson expects an answer and thus continues: "So, if I understand you correctly ..." The chairperson should repeat their statement and wait for a comment or its confirmation.
- The chairperson should only calm the discussion if necessary; they should settle any opposing opinions with a logical move for reconciliation: "Excuse me, is this in any way important to the development or success of our company?
- Board meeting participants should be able to explain WHY they think a certain way; it often happens that some participants don't really understand why something is important for the company. In very specific areas (most commonly in development), participants can be too focused on their projects and thus skip over the basics, which are key for the explanation; that's when other participants

don't fully understand. Here, the chairperson should ask sub-questions to get the basics right - otherwise, a good project might not get the support it deserves.
- Concluding a board meeting is the most important part. The chairperson should conclude the meeting in the following way: "Dear board meeting participants, with this decision I conclude today's board meeting. I think we we've been able to realise all the envisaged decisions within the period specified. I'd like to summarise today's decisions (using meaningful words and not getting into details that everyone has already heard). Colleague Xxx also suggested a discussion topic that I think is very important. All participants will receive their materials by - DATE (specify a date). The next board meeting will be held on - DATE (specify a date). The meeting's minutes can be found in the shared folder. I wish you all a very pleasant rest of the day.

Other participants should also have a say

As mentioned before, it's very important that every participant has a say as this is the only way to ensure the right results. After all, it's pointless inviting people to a board meeting who aren't relevant to the meeting in question. This is the main task and responsibility of the chairperson:
The chairperson should evenly divide the time allocated to each participant and should get the others to contribute. If nothing else works, they can try doing this by provoking them: "You're the expert in this field, why are the proposals the way they are, be very brief."
To a large extent, a board meeting is a meeting of one authority, who carries the highest responsibility, with their equivalent colleagues. That's a leader. I have to

stress that other people's words matter a great deal, and that they're not just words. All board meeting participants have to vote according to their conscience, since their vote becomes historic, i.e. it's co-deciding on the key issues in the company's development.

In addition to leading the board meeting participants, the chairperson also needs to motivate them, as this is the only way to reach successful conclusions. The chairperson should encourage the participants by creating a sense of personal responsibility and thereby increasing the chances of participants acting according to their conscience and implementing the board meeting's goals. They should continuously emphasise the "big picture" or the project's current vision since this will motivate the participants to make wise and responsible decisions.

7.6 PRACTICAL PART: YOU CAN'T DO EVERYTHING ON YOUR OWN

Task 1: *Write down five things that prove why a salesperson should know about company management.*

Task 2: *Write down an example of five-level leadership for your company.*

Task 3: *Write down the times allocated for your tasks within the company in one working week.*

Task 4: *Compose a board meeting for your company and your sales team.*

7.7 IN BRIEF: YOU CAN'T DO EVERYTHING ON YOUR OWN

1. Work distribution should follow sales processes.
2. One of the most important methods in the development of a sales department, and a company in general, is mentorship.
3. Leadership is an essential skill required by entrepreneurs.
4. Train a stock of leaders according to the five-level leadership programme.
5. Board meetings are the most important meeting for a company.
6. Their chairperson has a very responsible job.

8. COMPANY MANAGEMENT

Whenever people mention the term people management, others become hesitant thinking that it has something to do with manipulation. Every person has their talents and some are good at combining several different activities that lead to producing a certain solution or product. Engineers construct a product, marketing employees advertise it and salespeople sell it. But, all these "worlds" have to be combined in order to last and to be able to repeat the successful processes and thus earn the money needed for the development and life of the company. This combination is called company management.

8.1 COMPANY MANAGEMENT

When managing a company, all areas are important and their common goal is selling the solution or the product. That's why a company has to be managed with common goals and responsibility for the whole.

An excellent manager is able to explain to each business function, department and individual the company's direction and the importance of their work for meeting the set company goals. A charismatic person can motivate all the different views and characters towards the common goal - but everyone has to make a certain compromise and be even better in their daily work.

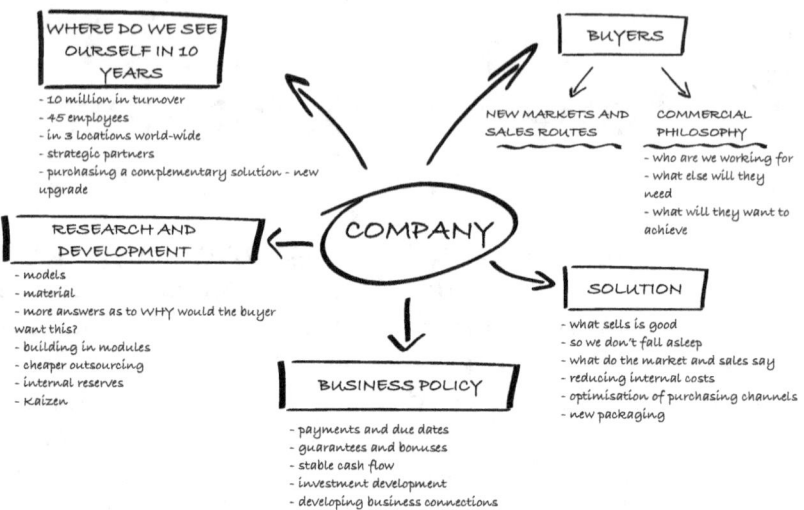

Mind map 14: Company

8.2 COMPANY DEVELOPMENT STRATEGY

The development strategy process is a process that happens in the entrepreneur's head. Most people don't even write down the information running around inside their head. And because of this, they have problems when they need to explain goals that exist solely in their head or manage a project and a company in this direction. As a professional business coach I come across this a lot, which led me to compose a system of steps that can be very useful in such cases:

1. Innovative: This includes short revelations that you should write down in your mobile phone or on a piece of paper and record whenever they appear. There are people who sit behind a desk in an office or at home racking their brains trying to think of an innovation. More often than not, this doesn't work. The worst suppressant of innovation is usually time we "don't have". New ideas occur spontaneously

when we're dealing with a problem that is really getting on our nerves, is physically straining or is taking money we urgently need somewhere else.
2. One extremely efficient method we have already mentioned is brainstorming, which is effective with several participants but is best performed with a moderator who ensures an orderly and cultural discussion. Generating ideas and alternatives is done concretely as an answer to the question posed. A motivational fact teaching us inventiveness says: "Look and you will find it."
3. Positive: Represents the advantages and values of an idea. It explains how the users will use it and what they will gain from it. You need to find a reason or an answer to the question: Why will this work? In what way will the innovation fit into the current solution for this area? Perhaps it is the process or concept that is the biggest added value and not the solution or product itself? A good example is nutritional supplements for weight loss used within groups, societies and clubs. The process or parallel effect of the concept is to encourage the participants to exercise regularly. We can conclude that the most important product is not the nutritional supplement; it is the motivation for regular physical activity.
4. Negative: Threats you face on the path to implementation. This could be legal restrictions, such as protection of personal data, licences for authorisation to work in a specific area, limitations set by the government etc. You need to think about the possible flaws in your ideas, which could be harmful or even dangerous to users, and, of course, check the legal facts so that your idea is not contrary to law.

5. Facts: The most efficient method is to check your answers to the right questions:
   - Where are we now?
   - What's our current condition? Analysis.
   - What do we have?
   - What don't we have?
   - What do we expect? A list.
   - What do we want to find out?
   - Where are the sources that could provide us with the information we're looking for?
   - What are our priorities? What do we need now?
6. Feelings: When we approach different people, we arouse different feelings. Some are insecure, bored, scared, angry, others are excited and optimistic. Feelings can't be measured nor excluded. It's important to talk about this at the start, before making a plan for implementing the project, process or the company itself. You need to talk about this and let every participant explain why they feel the way do. A vital process you need to learn and carry out over and over again is self-reflection; only a person who knows themselves very well can take on responsibility for the areas where they're the expert and not meddle with other participants.
7. Process: We've learned how we think and what the result of our activities will be. A plan or process has a defined goal, which is the central focus we always think about. You should write down your implementation plan in steps. Designate the managers responsible for individual tasks and the project manager or head of the company. It's crucial that you choose a manager who will ensure the timely execution of tasks and know how to motivate employees if something doesn't go as planned.

A project manager is responsible for your idea achieving its goal. They are responsible to the end users and all the team members, which is why you can expect high demands regarding the implementation of the tasks you were allocated. Conclusions are an important part of process management. Even if you haven't yet made a decision because you're missing some information, you can still reach a conclusion. Who will get the missing information and by when, immediate verification of what you've already achieved and what you'll do in the next short-term period, and are you following the time line outlined at the beginning? You also have to measure conclusions in this respect and determine if they have any side effects. You need to give innovations a chance to succeed - set a specific period, let's say at least six months or a year. If you give up on any agreed decisions that were defined as conclusions, this can lead to extensive damage and dissatisfaction among the participants of these activities. It's the manager's job to constantly reiterate the direction and the goals you wish to achieve and that the stated conclusions, i.e. milestones, are key for the next step in this direction.

8.3 A WORKING MANAGEMENT SYSTEM

Setting up a working system adapted to the management structure means that it corresponds to the size of the company, the management's culture and potentials, and the skill levels of the employees within the company. The first step is to prepare an organisation chart according to business functions or people; the way that the system is functioning now in practice. For each business function or person write down the tasks and responsibilities. The next step is to write down the processes; usually, the person who performs specific tasks does this. The indirect manager, head of department or company should set up the system using the steps of the processes. This means that all processes begin with facts and goals, workflows and warnings of possible mistake or dangers. Using analysis and a detailed overview of the processes and implementation, find any bottlenecks or the weak point where you've recorded the worst results. It's irrelevant if this is a mechanical error, human factor or any other kind of error. Anything that reduces the quality and thereby extends the process is relevant. Education is key for developing the leadership system. You can't expect a solution to arise just by thinking about what it was that brought you to this situation. You need to activate all the possibilities in all the areas of the company. If you work out the processes in production and establish efficient management, mistakes can occur due to the "outdated" functioning of other business functions. As has been shown in practice, you need to plan well and begin patiently and slowly. Here, I don't mean years, but months; otherwise, your company's competitive advantage or ability to stay on the market could completely disappear. You need to start at the top, by not training "totalitarian" managers, but mentors. The most efficient transition from an old style system to a more efficient system is to tolerantly suggest and develop wider views. When a company grows from a small company, organisational segments are created according to a "one for all" principle. When the number of orders increases and new technological solutions have to be implemented and additional human resources employed, things get complicated by not allocating responsibilities to co-workers and by constant supervision on behalf of the manager or the company's founder.

The "old system" that worked in the small company

doesn't divide business functions according to the processes, people and responsibilities in the big one; that's why it's often a major suppressant of the company's growth. It's completely inefficient and self-destructing to comment on the incompetence of your colleagues. If they seem unmotivated, analyse why that's the case. If you make use of the practices mentioned, I advise you stop and read the chapter on development strategies again. Start making changes immediately since you're harming the company and, in the long-term, also yourself.

The transition and upgrade of a systemic company or project management means organising a mentorship system. In other words, start training leaders before they become them.

8.4 CONTROLLING

The word "control" sounds really unfriendly when people use it in their private lives. Do you remember my description of a control freak, i.e. a person who wants to know and decide on everything in a company, in the previous chapter? I wouldn't wish this kind of stress on anyone since there are alternative and better solutions in the form of managing processes.

Salespeople often react angrily when the managing director demands a report from them. If your company uses CRM (customer relationship management), you can simply print the reports or copy them to a table and forward it to your superior.

First and foremost, reports are intended for self-control. I'm sure it often happens that you've been working all day, but have nothing to show for it. This is a good reason to find help or new knowledge in the field of time management.

8.5 REPORTING

Mind map 15: Reporting

Ask yourself: "Why does management need reports?" Simply to make the right decisions. As said in the chapter on meetings and board meetings, only the right (exact and correct) information can bring about the right decisions, which are preconditions for the successful future of any company. Financial statements (monthly, weekly, daily) are key information for the manager or the managing director. The sales situation can tell us what we can expect and when we'll receive the funds for the solutions sold and deals closed. Reports can also clarify the condition of production, quality control, overtime, multi-shift work etc. - these are just a few details that will position you on the market either among the competitive or the uncompetitive players.

Reports are seen by most people (those that have to prepare them) as a waste of time and something terrible; in the times we're living in, alternative ways can be found, i.e. programmes and applications that facilitate this work. If your manager is extremely conservative and "rolls their eyes" when seeing the price of software, but you feel that such a purchase would really simplify your work, your team should calculate an ROI (return on investment) and present it to them. In other words: "sell" the idea and write it down in numbers (money) to show the calculated loss the company is experiencing on account of not using modern tools.

8.6 SELLING THE COMPANY AS AN EXIT STRATEGY

There are many reasons why companies finish operating, and selling the company is one of them. Selling the company is often referred to as the owner's exit strategy. Reasons for selling can include:

- The entrepreneur no longer sees any added value in this business.
- The owner feels like they have given it their all.
- The company limits the owner in reaching higher goals.
- Something happened that can't be fixed.
- A strategic decision. If you're about to sell your company, verify and think about the following facts:
- Contemplate whether you've made a final decision and how it will affect the business and your employees.
- What are the conclusions of the SWOT analysis?
- »Sum up« the pros and cons of your decision.
- Find someone who could benefit from your company or whose primary business could be supplemented by your company.
- The minimum sale price shouldn't be less than the annual turnover and the value of the fixed

assets.
- Establish the company's solution base.
- Establish the company's supplier base.
- Establish the company's buyer base.
- Examine long-term contracts.
- Make sure your financial data is transparent.
- Write down the work processes according to business functions.
- Combine everything in a detailed expert report (implementation plan).
- Prepare a long-term plan with clear numerical and financial data.
- Answer the following question: "Why should someone buy the company and what will they gain from it?
- Find at least five potential buyers.
- Hold meetings gradually, don't offer everything at once.

Selling a company is an established practice in big companies in order to maintain financial brokerage companies that deal in shares and stock-exchange transactions. The primary consideration is to implement the investors' financial contribution since, as is known, investors are never intensively involved in the company's operation in such ways. Such cases are not as common in privately owned or smaller companies. A change in ownership structure in smaller private companies most frequently occurs due to a transition of generations within a family or due to poor business results or bankruptcy. Strategic mergers or takeovers by multinational companies are fewer, since the big system and its rigidity usually ruin otherwise adaptable and inventive smaller companies.

My experience in selling companies includes six separate cases in which I'd founded the company (small and micro companies), developed it to a profitable functionality and later sold it to new owners. I believe there are only two options in the segment of small companies: "life or death". It rarely happens that one of the founders or owners decides to sell their company, since they see it as "their baby". For me, this was a special challenge. When I got bored of the routine and lack of long-term vision, I found a buyer and sold them the idea and the company. It wasn't easy since the buyers didn't buy anything at that moment. I also made several mistakes along the way, which is one of the reasons why you're reading this book. One of its purposes is to prevent you, the readers, from making the same sales mistakes that I did. These are facts that result from my experiences and, as such, I don't want them to be a taboo topic. If you run out of ideas and energy to develop your company further, sell it and establish a new one. Long-term persistence on bygone methods will lead you to failure and poor health. Companies fail due to poor cash flow, not due to insufficient progress. Companies that make a profit often also have difficulties with payments, which leads them to their downfall.

My guiding principle, dictated by my experiences, is: Don't offer help unless they ask you for it. I can list quite a few companies, owned by people I know, that failed, even though I could see from afar what they were missing. When I was younger I often got smacked round the head by my own sympathetic naivety, since entrepreneurs rarely saw my criticism as well-intentioned. An entrepreneur is a very confident and incisive person; they have to be, otherwise they'd find it difficult to succeed on the market. In their heads they have a plan B for a problem's resolution, and someone else with their own suggestions can quickly destroy the "only" direction that they had envisaged.

A company that lingers on principles that the changing market and buyer demands have made outdated always ends up in trouble. I remember a company that went bankrupt. The basic business idea was excellent. Through a friend of mine, the owners had asked me if I could help them. I gave them some very brief advice to stop mistreating their buyers, to promise only what they could deliver and to keep their promises. A very simple sentence that could have proven to be the solution for the company, regardless of its financial situation. Even though it's true, this sentence bore no fruit because of the owners' resentment and damaged ego.

It's definitely better to sell such a company and "thrive" in a new one. To see selling the company as something bad is as naive as not starting a company if we know what we'd be doing and we truly want this to happen.

8.7 THE NAKED TRUTH: AN EXAMPLE OF SELLING A COMPANY

Below I describe two examples of selling a company that are very different in their business functions and missions. Through them, I'd like to bring selling a company closer to you - as an exit strategy, and show you that it's nothing hard or bad, but just a sale as such.

- Reasons for selling a transportation company:

1. The organisation and the advanced distribution system have reached financial efficiency break-even point.
2. When the company was optimised to the level of complete repetitions, it should've been expanded to 50 or more lorries, which was financially practically impossible at that time.
3. The transportation company was the first step in my business career as I didn't have any financial means to get started. I was never really interested in the transportation industry.
4. With regards to efficiency and a relatively

good sale price the difference after paying all the costs was too small.

- Reasons for selling a maternity clothing shop:

  1. Organising activities in my own business premises.
  2. I had the idea when my wife was pregnant for the second time; pregnant women often feel nauseous while driving, and there was no such shop nearby.
  3. Successful cooperation with a supplier, who later expanded their activity to several shops in Slovenia which contributed to the value of the company.
  4. My wife was no longer pregnant so I didn't see the potential in my ideas for further developing the company.

Selling a company is a demanding decision and a great challenge. Don't sell the company if you don't have a detailed plan as to where you'll invest the funds received from selling it. After selling the company, take time to rest and think about the future. This is also an important part of creating a new company. Remember, a "battery powered dog" with empty batteries doesn't bark very loudly - even though your entrepreneurial soul will already be very bored on the third or fourth day of your "holiday". When selling a company, make sure you carefully observe its surroundings, i.e. other companies on the market and the movement of their ownership capital. Some companies merge for various reasons. The "healthiest" merging methods are joint projects, acting on the market or developing complementary technologies.

Some entrepreneurs hire external experts to sell their company. In such cases, an internal evaluation of the company is performed and the potential in its future development is estimated. The company is worth as much as its weakest link. The biggest hurdle, which is often also the reason why a responsible owner starts thinking about selling or finding a strategic partner, is the mentality of the people within the company. Often, there is not enough ambition within such a company to look for new products, new buyers and markets, and there's insufficient focus on the area in which the company is most successful. Usually, there's also a lack of desire for general improvement and progress of the people within the company. When the general mood is low because of inefficient leadership or direction, even the most positive or ambitious employees "pull back", since their ideas are always trampled on or go otherwise unheard.

The thinking that has brought us to selling the company, cannot miraculously make things better. Once we've realised this, we normally start to think about "change management" on the basis of the previously mentioned evaluation. It has happened quite a few times that by introducing changes, owners who detected problems in their company, but refused external help from advisers and other professionals, saw the light at the end of the tunnel and withdrew from the sale. The distribution achieved according to business functions, together with a clear vision and responsibility, and suitably worked-out processes and work intensity turn out to be an excellent opportunity for a company's new drive. If the decision to sell the company remains unchanged, there's a good chance that the company can get a much higher sale value than it would have done otherwise.

If you decide to sell your company, it's important that you follow a process that is logical in sales. In the chapter on sales tools we talked about steps that always happen or should happen when selling a company.

Company Management

- A tested system should always start with a list of potential buyers of the company.
- Write down the list regardless of whether you know the future buyer or not.
- Think about what activity has similar (the same) buyers as your company.
- From the line of business move on to concrete names of companies in the vicinity with which you could close the deal.
- Using your list of potential buyers, check connections with other companies. If you don't do that, you might be surprised to see later that one of those companies already owns a company similar to yours.
- When you contact potential buyers, make sure you've thoroughly prepared your protocol since just one misrepresented thought could threaten the deal.
- It's crucial that you check the balance sheets from the last few years and the structure of the movement of employees within the company. Don't be fooled by turnover growth as it makes sense that a company can grow by up to twenty percent without expanding much as it's using internal reserves. If you're not very knowledgeable in the field of analyses, I suggest you talk to a verified expert since this is a difficult decision where you can make irreparable mistakes.
- Make sure a potential buyer doesn't notice your weaknesses; otherwise, they might decide to ruin you as your competitor and take over your business, which will leave you with nothing.
- Meetings with selected potential buyers should be carefully prepared and should take place on business premises. I advise against holding

meetings in a café or something similar.
- Try to keep the news about selling the company a secret.
- A business meeting regarding the sale of a company is a serious issue; you need to ensure the necessary intimacy and reduce the possibility of "disturbances" at the meeting. The best turnout of the meeting is the potential buyer's suggestion of a merger.

When first meeting the potential buyer of your company, you will usually stir their interest and a quiet desire to buy your company. That's why pre-preparation is so significant - the potential buyer mustn't find out whether you're weak in any areas of your business.

When selling your company, you'll always be asking yourself: "Why would someone buy my company if they have their own?" Answers to this question are simple:

1. So that they can take over your buyers in the market.
2. So that they gain your know-how, patents or excellent employees or experts.

That's how successful entrepreneurs think. Those who want to buy your company just because of the excellent balance sheets are not real buyers and will probably close the company eventually. The realisation that you know the reasons why your buyer would buy what you're offering is the most important thing also when selling your company. The processes related to selling a company aren't usually short, as you need to be attentive to many details. Mistakes that can happen can encourage the buyer to take over your company free-of-charge.

If you have sold your company, think thoroughly about what you are going to do now. Many entrepreneurs decide to embark on business adventures beyond their field of business, expertise or general abilities. This usually leads to failure as it's difficult to return to past glories.

8.8 PRACTICAL PART: COMPANY MANAGEMENT

Task 1: *Write down five skills necessary for a good leader.*

Task 2: *Write down three past sales situations in your company. Write down how you would've managed them.*

Task 3: *Write down an example of your daily report.*

Task 4: *In ten points, write down the steps you would take if you were to sell your company.*

8.9 IN BRIEF: COMPANY MANAGEMENT

1. All areas are important when managing a company.
2. Don't underestimate the process of the company's development strategy.
3. Reporting and controlling are indispensable to the successful development of a company.
4. View the selling of a company the same way as selling solutions; prepare well for it and don't persist with an existing company if you think it's pointless.

CONCLUSION

IN SALES YOU NEED TO GET "NAKED"

Mind map 16: Naked sales

Throughout the entire book you have probably realised what is suggested by its title. In these times of "cloud" computing and artificial intelligence, it has become clear even in more traditional industries that due to such fast development in all branches of industry their sales foundations will have to be changed. This book attempts to present this through practice, which is and will become even more important in the future when most of our work will be done by machines and computers, and as a result people will be paid only for results. This will be even more evident in sales services. As you've learned sales is no "bogeyman", but it's also not a industry that can be "neglected". It's a fact that more "precise" robots won't be able to substitute most of the salesperson's practical skills, particularly their relationships with people, for some time. You also learned that the point of sales is to close them, and that most of the other processes aren't important as long as that is effective. Complete practice is the essence of modern sales, that's why you have to become completely "naked" in the process, and thus motivate your buyer. During the internet revolution, buyers have become well-prepared as they can easily check every bit of information on the solution you're selling and its price. It's important that your mentality follows suit. You also need to understand that traditional "persuasion" no longer suffices to sell complex solutions. In addition to traditional sales methods, every sales activity needs to be well advocated from a sentence to a meeting, since this is the only way to persuade your buyers to buy and to maintain your good name.

As you've learned, sales need to be made naked in their key parts, i.e. closings. Many sales advisers might smirk at the principles of this book, but no one can deny its essence - sales in practice.

As an entrepreneur I'm sure you've dealt with sales advisers and "coaches". Most of you probably weren't satisfied on at least one occasion. You've probably said to yourself too many times: "Make the sale instead of me or teach me how to sell in practice, I don't need advice as to how to sell, I just want to sell and develop the company further." It's important to emphasise that no one will sell instead of you in your company, and you won't succeed without practice.

Even though you might say I'm spitting in the wind, I can tell you that you will recognise a good salesperson by wanting to link their payment to their results. Often, this will cost you more than employing a sales representative or specialist salesperson, but this is the better solution in the long-term.

AM I A SALES PROPHET IN MY HOMETOWN?

In the internet times of complete globalisation you should view the global market as your local market. Your ideas and business operations shouldn't be limited by national and geographical boundaries. It has happened too many times that an individual's entrepreneurial potential wasn't recognised in their home town and country. Think about this when employing salespeople and other employees. Don't be constrained by racial, national or similar reservations. Try to recognise the potential in people, whether they are agents in a foreign market or your neighbours. But... Don't live with the excuses of a poor domestic market.
Think globally at home as well, and you'll realise that your domestic market is also part of the global economy and it doesn't think much differently.
If you wish to become a "sales prophet in your home town", be exactly that: a "prophet". An important fact, stated by many globally renowned entrepreneurs, is that in every business you have to gamble. Gamble several years in advance. Only in this way will you stay ahead of the competition, will your ideas bear great fruit and will you fulfil your biggest dreams.

I too wish to fulfil my dreams. As you've learned from this book, part of them is to help people fulfil theirs. Since I wanted to spare you some of the scars usually caused by business life, I decided to share my experiences with you. I'm not the first, nor will I be the last, who wishes to transfer a good, wrong, sometimes miraculous and generally wonderful life to those who have got stuck on an obstacle on their business path or wish to succeed in business one day. It's important for every entrepreneur or future entrepreneur to monitor the writings of business and life's history, and to follow all the up-to-date information available in these modern times that can be obtained from people. I sometimes hear the excuse my buyers, clients or friends make: "You know, we're in a crisis right now." But my answer is always the same: "But you live here and now. This is your opportunity."

You've read a book that will significantly change your business achievements or your view of the business world. You've learned about life methods where you were able to say "I'm excellent in this area" and were able to awaken the "sleeping potential" in other segments that you've always kept hidden away.

The mission I set out to achieve by writing this book is simple. My first goal was to encourage people to take a step forwards towards happiness and to start living the life that they deserve. My other goal was to write a book that you would really read, as I believe it will have fulfilled you, at least a little bit. I have huge respect for every reader. Those who sensed any personal criticism in this book, understand that it wasn't me who wrote it, but Life. Don't be too hard on yourself! Too many people take their work too seriously. With responsibility to their actions and future visions but not enough bravery and relaxation they, unfortunately, block the potential within themselves and those closest to them.

The central message I wanted to get across is:

- Ask your potential buyers questions.
- Ask yourself questions.
- Answer your questions.
- Become someone's coach.
- Hire a coach for yourself.
- Love your buyers.
- Love your colleagues.
- Thank your family and closest friends for their support and patience.

Even if you put the tested methods and tools into practice, it won't always be pleasant. Sometimes, it will be hard and tiresome. That's why you should never forget your dreams and goals. Dreaming isn't forbidden and you can never outgrow it.

I am and will always be this way, since helping others reach higher goals is my passion. I always rely on my personal motto: Heal the past, live the present and dream the future.

WELCOME TO THE WORLD OF EXPERIENCE AND QUALITY SINCE 1976

NOVAK EXHAUST SYSTEMS SLOVENIA

„OFFER YOUR CAR BEST QUALITY"

S E A F A R I N G
Y A C H T S

www.ingramcontent.com/pod-product-compliance
Lightning Source LLC
Chambersburg PA
CBHW071052240526
45471CB00015B/1705